Three Years
Behind
The Guns

The search-light in action.

Three Years Behind the Guns

THE TRUE CHRONICLES OF A "DIDDY-BOX"

by
John B. Tisdale

Illustrated by
Chris Jörgensen and George Varian
and with vintage photographs

Arx Publishing
Merchantville, New Jersey
2017

This edition published by
Arx Publishing
Merchantville, New Jersey

Originally published by
The Century Company
New York, 1908.

This Edition

ISBN: 978-1-935228-17-2

To
Every man who has walked
the decks of a man-of-war.

CONTENTS

Chapter   Page

LIST OF ILLUSTRATIONS

PREFACE

May 1, 1898 is often cited as the exact date when the United States of America transformed from a relatively minor regional power to a bona fide player on the world stage. On that day, the U.S. Asiatic Squadron under Commodore George Dewey in his flagship *Olympia*, utterly destroyed the fleet of the fast-fading Spanish empire at Manila Bay in the Philippines.

Though it was penned during these heady days, *Three Years Behind the Guns* is not so much a chronicle of this turning point in history as it is the unique perspective of one very young sailor on the events leading up to it. It is a pithy memoir of life aboard a man-o'-war as the age of "wooden ships and iron men" was giving way to the era of big guns, heavy steel, and high speed. Of these new ships, the protected cruiser *Olympia* was both a prototype and an outstanding example. Though our author is the main protagonist of this memoir, *U.S.F.S. Olympia* is the leading lady.

Little is known about the author of *Three Years Behind the Guns*. On the earliest editions of the book, he is listed cryptically as "L. G. T." In later editions, he is identified as "Lieu Tisdale." A check of *Olympia's* crew roster*

---

*The crew roster may be found in Galt, William W. (1904). *The Battle of Manila Bay: An Epic Poem*, Norfolk, VA, p. 76

at Manila Bay, however, reveals no one of that precise name. Instead, there is a listing for "John B. Tisdale, Landsman." This is probably our fellow, given that within the book itself, he is addressed on numerous occasions as "Jack" by his shipmates, a Japanese girl, and even by himself while soliloquizing. The reason he chose to publish the book anonymously is unknown.

Since the days of Ulysses, sailors have been known for their tall-tales, and our Jack is no exception. His numerous anecdotes sparkle with wit and verve, even when they sound suspiciously apocryphal. The reader will find literal fish-stories here—such as when Jack captures a two-foot-long flying fish on the deck or when a shipmate nearly loses a toe while doing some illicit angling. But there are also descriptions of more somber events that are easily verified by outside sources, such as the death Coxswain John Johnson who was killed during gunnery practice, and the wreck of the steamer *On-Wo* with the loss of 255 passengers and crew. Jack and his Olympian crewmates pulled 38 survivors from the water and were commended for their efforts.

Perhaps the most impressive thumbs-up for the memoir's authenticity comes from none other than Admiral Dewey himself, the hero of Manila Bay. In an antique advertisement,* the admiral provides a generous endorsement of the book, saying: "Many of my friends and I have read it with the greatest interest. I can vouch for many of the facts; and the description of the Battle of Manila Bay is one of the best I have ever seen published. The type and active life of our American seamen is well and interestingly portrayed, and the book is well worth

*The Publishers' Weekly, October 10, 1908, page 980

the attention of both young and old."

When originally published in 1908—ten years after the battle—Jack's anonymous memoir met with critical acclaim. *The New York Times* called it: "An intimate record of life aboard an American man-of-war, and is written with such detail, vivacity, and the knack for vivid expression that it keeps one turning pages until the last one is reached. This Jackie has keen eyes and quick ears, and can put the things he saw and thought about into particularly vigorous English."*

The New York Observer added: "Though sufficiently simple and direct in style to hold the interest of the young reader, this book will be found by grown-ups to be absorbing as a novel."†

When first published, the book was billed as a behind-the-scenes look at life aboard a modern American warship at a time when the U.S. was building giant dreadnought battleships by the dozen and recruiting thousands of young fellows to man them. But time and technology were flying by and within another decade, the catastrophe of the Great War had thrown into eclipse the comparatively minor incident of the Spanish-American War. The subsequent epic struggle of World War II with its colossal ships, ocean-spanning battles and city-shattering weapons made Dewey's victory at Manila Bay seem as ancient and obscure as Trafalgar or Salamis.

I believe that the modern reader, particularly the student of history, will find *Three Years Behind the Guns*

The New York Times Saturday Review of Books and Art, September 19, 1908, page 32.

†*The New York Observer*, October 1, 1908, page 437

even more captivating than the reader of 110 years ago. For young folks of today whose grandparents were born during the 1950s, reading about life aboard a warship from the 1890s is like visiting an old Victorian mansion. If you've toured Dewey's *Olympia* in Philadelphia where she exists to this day, you know that is a literal truth. The lovely dark wood paneling and antique furniture in the officers' quarters contrasts sharply with the painted steel and spartan decks of the crew areas, and the grime and oppressive atmosphere of the engineering spaces. This is the scene where the authentic "steam punk" of Tisdale's story plays out, complete with coming-of-age hijinks, grinding machinery, clouds of black smoke and moments of profound contemplation.

Like *Olympia* herself, *Three Years Behind the Guns* is a hybrid—part solid fact, part work of art. Both ship and book are unique historical artifacts, which is one of the reasons we have decided to donate a portion of the sales of this book to the continuing upkeep of *U.S.F.S. Olympia* and her steward, the Independence Seaport Museum in Philadelphia. Such beautiful mementos deserve to be maintained if for no other reason than as concrete reminders of how we got here.

We are thrilled to publish a new edition of this classic work in a format that will be easily accessible for modern readers. Save for some minor editing and the addition of a few footnotes, the text is practically untouched from the original. Jack's unique voice and witty observations come through loud and clear as they did over a century before. His vivid account breathes life into *Olympia*, which he knew not as a retired museum ship, but as the powerful, hardy seahawk she was in her prime. "The flag-ship is a thing alive," he wrote. "It has parts and being. We have heard it breathe, and who will question that in Captain Reed, it has both brain and soul?"

Tisdale originally dedicated *Three Years Behind the Guns* to "every man who has walked the decks of a man-of-war." We would like to dedicate this new edition to the repose of the soul of John B. Tisdale in particular. He was a man who not only walked the decks, but who recorded his impressions with such trenchant good humor and eloquent detail, that people a century and more afterwards might feel as if they are walking along right beside him.

Indeed, if you ever find yourself aboard *Olympia*, go and look for him. You may glimpse his shade still standing faithfully at his post—behind the guns.

—*Anthony P. Schiavo, Jr.*
Merchantville, NJ
July, 2017

THREE YEARS BEHIND
THE GUNS

CHAPTER I

U.S.F.S. *Olympia*,
San Francisco Bay,
Thursday, August 8, 1895.

"Tell your troubles to a policeman," runs the saw. Would that I might, or to any other man on terra-firma! But if there is on this great globe one place where man hides his light under a bushel, it is on a man-of-war. Here nobody asks nor answers "Why?" to other questions than, "Where do you hail from?" And while there are hundreds of fellows about me, apparently content, and even delighted with this state of affairs, I am so hungry for companionship that, to avert heart-starvation, I am forced into the writing of another diary.—Come off, Jackie! You're not a school-boy any longer, but a landlubber on board a man-of-war, and this is your log. Here will you bring your joys and your sorrows, just as you used to carry them to your mother. Dear little Momsie, how her heart is aching tonight! And I....Cut it out, boy!—the past, home, and all that sacred word implies.

My new life began a month and a half ago, when I ran away to sea and boarded the *Independence*, with nine other applicants (all strangers to one another), for the United States Navy. Even as I write, the cold chills return and chase up and down my spine, recalling to me an officer whose ferocity of mien has won for him the nickname of "The Bulldog." Perhaps he is just the man for the place; as with a watch-dog, when you see him growling at the porter's lodge, you are at liberty to turn back or to face the terror. I had chosen a name to enlist under; but when the Bulldog growled, "What's your name?" I positively forgot it, and up and told him on the spot the name given me by my sponsors in baptism, together with the one I have inherited from many generations of Americans. Once I had spoken it, the tension was relieved; and when he asked me what I was qualified to do, I asked him to give me something on deck.

From him we were passed on to the doctor, whose greeting was: "Come on, come on, strip off; let's see what you're made of."

We stripped, and went through an examination that was first cousin to hazing. Some he kept longer than others, and when I saw a bulky Irish man, who weighed one hundred and eighty, come back with his card marked "Rejected," I thought of my one hundred and thirty-two pounds, and my heart sank. But of the ten only three were accepted, and I am one of them.

We all dressed and went above, where the officer-of-the-deck called out: "Those who have been accepted by the doctor lay aft to the captain and be sworn in."

The captain was promenading the poop-deck. When we came into his presence he stepped to the capstan and took from it a small, well-

The capstan.

worn Bible (I wonder if it was the same his mother gave

him when he went away to Annapolis), which he held in his hand, and, folding his arms across his breast, told us to hold up our right hands; then asked our names, country, birthplace, were we married, had we been in jail, etc. Then briefly reciting the articles of war, he asked: "Do you realize the importance of the oath you are about to take?"

Three affirmatives came short and quick. The captain lifted the Bible in his right hand, and the oath was taken which makes me for three years a sailor. In a fatherly manner the captain then spoke to us, bidding us endeavor to be good boys, a credit to our country, and a pride to the ship we sailed.

With this admonition, we were turned over to a sailor they called "Jack-o-the-dust" (I wonder why "o-the-dust") and we followed "Dust" below.

In the store-room I found a man whose time had expired. He was about my size, and I presented him with the suit I was wearing. He put it on with evident pride (it was almost new, and had cost Dad forty-five dollars), and I watched him walk down the gang-plank. Just for a second I wished I were in those clothes again, but "Out of sight, out of mind," and, turning at "attention," I was fitted out with everything a sailor needs—from needles and thread to:

One hammock, with mattress;
Three mattress-covers;
One pair white blankets;
Two blue flannel suits of clothes;
Three white duck suits of clothes;
Two white cap-covers;

Two blue caps;
One watch cap;
One suit oilskins;
Two neckerchiefs;
Two suits underwear;
Two pair navy shoes;
Six pair socks;
Blacking and brush;
Bowl, cup, and plate of white agate-ware with blue
    bands, and U.S.N. in blue on each piece;
Knife, fork, and spoon;
One pea-jacket;
    And last, but not least—
One Diddy-box.

A Diddy-box!—The sanctum sanctorum of Uncle Sam's Navy. Only yesterday I heard a lesson on its sacredness, as one man berated another until every adjective in his vocabulary was worn to tatters, when he arose to the convincing climax: "Why, that man is low enough to go through a shipmate's diddy-box!"

Dressed in my uniform, with the rest of my chattels tied in a canvas bag, I was turned loose on the deck of the *Independence*. From innate modesty, I held my shirt together at the throat, and stood wondering (The two who enlisted with me I have never recognized to this day.) At that moment, I believe I would have bartered all I had, to have turned Time's wheel backward for just one week; but while I stood thus, half bewildered, a fellow walked up with extended hand and said: "Duke me, kid!" From his gesture I knew it was a hand-shake and responded. He said: "I see you've made it. Are you going

The *Independence.*

The "Diddy-box."

on the *Olympia?*" I answered that I hoped so.

The fates so ordained it that before sundown of the day of my enlistment, my hope was realized, as I was one of fifty who were drafted from the *Independence* to the *Olympia*.

On the cutter that brought us over, we were each given a ticket. Mine read:

U.S.F.S. *Olympia*

Watch. . . . . Starboard
Division . . . . Second
Gun . . . . Aft Turret No. I
Boat . . . . Whale 22
Mess . . . . No. 3
Battalion Co. . . . . No. 3
Ship No., hammock, and bag 2149

A careful perusal left me almost as enlightened as a Dutchman would be with a Chinese guidebook. But the chap who had extended to me the glad hand in the morning was at my elbow, and said: "Show me your billet." Just a glance, and he said: "You are all right; you are right next to me, and I will help you until you get started."

And so he has, from that hour up to the present. I have christened him Handy Andy, for he is the handiest article I have known since my first knife. My first knife! It had eight blades, including a button-hook, a saw and a corkscrew. As I recall it now, it weighed a pound, and was a gift from Santa Claus. How compares it with the single blade Uncle Sam has given me, and which now hangs from my lanyard?

But back to Andy. He is heart from his cap-band to his shoe-soles; and though he speaks a vernacular that at first was difficult to recognize as English, I find it unique, and would gladly reproduce it in writing if I could; but to say "goil" for girl, and "loidy" for lady, is such a feeble imitation, I shall not attempt it. "Tough?" Not one bit of it. He came from New York City, has served his apprenticeship, and this is his second cruise probably as much as I shall ever know about his past. He knows everything, and has hinted to me that there are no "stairs," but ladders, on ships, and that it is always either "above" or "below." There are not four "stories" to the ship; but a torpedo-deck, berth-deck, gun-deck, and a spar-deck. Many more are the things he has told me, but I cannot remember, nor understand half of them yet; but one bit of advice was, "When them guys with the swords and buttons ask you anything, don't know nothing. If you tell them you do, you'll get a call-down; 'cause, you see, they'll tell you Uncle Sam is paying them to tell you that"

Acting on this advice, when asked if I knew anything of military tactics, I answered, "Not much," and was placed in the awkward squad; but being unable to hide four years training in a military academy, was soon promoted to the ranks, and with the blue-jackets marched in the Fourth of July parade. It was a novel sensation to be on exhibition on Van Ness Avenue, in San Francisco. I was not looking for familiar faces, but from the pavement, whence came the cheering, I thought I caught a glimpse of golden hair and a pair of blue eyes looking surprised and inquiringly. I wonder if she recognized me?

While there is small fear that I shall ever forget, I

think it proper, in writing a log, that I should record my first difficulty.

It occurred on the morning of June 25. To sleep in a hammock under the trees where you can throw your leg over the side and find firm footing, is very different from having it swung so high that you can touch the ceiling with your hands, and be entirely out of the way of the tallest man on board as he walks the deck. The fear of falling and breaking my neck had kept me awake all night. At five o'clock in the morning, I was rousted out. I got into my new uniform, but *could not* fix my hammock. Andy, to the rescue, said: "I'll lash up for you today, kid; don't be discouraged; in a month you will take to it like you take to your Jimokey."

I asked him what Jimokey was, and he seemed surprised that I did not know it to mean Jamaica-coffee.

At nine o'clock, having eaten my breakfast, I stood wondering where Andy was. Everybody seemed employed; but all sailors looked alike to me, so I smoked and waited until startled into a cold perspiration by hearing my name shouted as from a megaphone, and I was hurried before the officer-of-the-deck. I found him fairly writhing with rage; he paced the deck, swung his arms, and roared; then going to the gun-rack, he wrote something in his report-book. While all this was going on I stood as speechless as a wooden Indian in front of a cigar shop. The details are lost; but I went to Mare Island, where I worked all day, like a—a—a—, well, a man-of-war's-man!

Every Saturday morning at eleven o'clock they hold what is termed "The Stick." The captain is judge, the accuser is the prosecuting attorney, and you are your own lawyer. Andy had remarked at breakfast that I was down for a chance, and wanted to know what I was going to do. I told him, "Nothing."

"That won't do," said Andy. "Just lay low until you get before the skipper, then give him the straight goods, but cut it short"

In answer to my name, I stepped before the captain, and uncovered. With a grave look he told me I was reported for neglect of duty—shirking and inattention to the bugle call. A charge like this is serious enough to send a man to the Island, but when I told him I did not know there had been a bugle call, he plied me with questions until he found I had been on ship less than twenty-four hours. Then the cloud passed from his face and he excused me, but reprimanded my accuser for not having looked into the matter before reporting me.

The *Olympia* is a protected cruiser with a main battery of four 8-inch guns, and ten 5-inch rapid-fire guns; secondary battery, fourteen 6-pounders, and six 1-pounder rapid-fire guns, and four gatlings.

I belong to the aft Turret-gun No. 1, and my hammock swings in the first row aft in the starboard gangway on the gun-deck. From it I catch fleeting glimpses into the captain's cabin. It is indeed his castle; for there he eats, sleeps, and holds court. The captain of a man-of-war! Who on earth is to compare with him? Not a king, nor an emperor. His power is absolute!

To minister to his personal comforts, he has an orderly (a marine), a steward, a cook, and a cabin-boy. His table is spread with Irish linen, and laid with Sèvres china, cut crystal, and sterling silver; but, unless presiding at a banquet, he takes his meals like a hermit—absolutely alone.

But there are twenty-two messes on board. One of them, Mess No. 3, is on the starboard side of the gun-deck. From the ceiling there hangs, on a wire cable, a wooden table immaculate from frequent scrubbings, but quite bare of linen. Three times a day it is pulled down, and the benches that are folded on top of it are placed alongside. Near by there is a mess-locker, which contains almost everything to be found in a well-regulated larder, or pantry. Below the locker hang a dish-pan, a bread-tub, and two "breakers"—one for vinegar, the other for molasses. This is where I take my meals. There are twenty-one of us. We laugh and joke; but we are creating a new comradeship, and not for—? Well, I know this much: I have no desire to be a captain of a man-of-war.

Last week, with the Naval-inspector on board, we went to San Diego on our official trial trip. The *Olympia's* contract calls for a speed of twenty knots, but for eight hours she logged 22.6—the fastest time ever made on the Pacific. There is a fine, modern patent log aboard; but for all that we held the reel each hour, and took the time with chips and glass, just as it was done by the earliest navigator.

Off San Diego, we had target practice. The 8-inch turret guns—the only ones about which there seemed to be any question—proved themselves all right; but the 5-inch gun, Battery No. 4, on port side, because of her recoil cylinder not being properly filled, jumped out of her carriage, pinning Coxswain J—* to the deck, and instantly killing him. This ended target practice second. We weighed anchor almost immediately. The dead

*This incident refers to Coxswain John Johnson who was killed during gunnery practice on April 30, 1895.

coxswain was wrapped in the union-jack and placed upon a bier under the after bridge of the spar-deck; and with a sentry of blue-jackets standing guard, he was carried back to Mare Island, where, with naval honors, he was committed to the earth.

A touching tribute to his memory, a sketch of the tragedy and an accompanying poem, both the work of shipmates, has been neatly put into print, and distributed among the crew.

On our return trip, as we were casting anchor at Sausalito, a boatswain had his leg cut off. It must be events like these, coupled with the knowledge that we are soon to sail on a long cruise to the Orient, that make a fellow think of things he is trying to forget.

Well, Diddy, we have had a long confab tonight, and I feel better. We will probably not have so exhaustive a seance again; but tomorrow night, between eight and nine, I shall bring you here on this mess-chest, and have a little chat with you. And so on each day, I hope, until June 24, 1898.

U. S. F. S. *Olympia*, Friday, August 9, 1895.

Have been aboard one month and a half, and have made more blunders today than I did the first week. Can it be because my mind has been wending backward?

August 10th.

"And the old, old story is told again at five o'clock in the morning." For then the big gun booms; the bell strikes two; the bugle sings: "I can't get 'em up—I can't get 'em up." The boatswain pipes, then in a thunderous voice drawls out, "A-l-l hands—up, a-l-l hammocks—, come on—, roust out— lash and carry!" This is the song of the merry chanter, as out we tumble. In eight minutes we are dressed, hammocks lashed, and stowed in a netting on the spar-deck; then back to our "jimock"—a cup of coffee taken standing. At half past five again the boatswain pipes, and thunders the order: "A-l-l hands . . . turn to and scrub the decks with sand; a-l-l hands scrub all white paint and clean all bright work."

At half past seven each man gets a bucket of fresh water, strips to the waist line and takes a sailor's bath. His towel he hangs on a line; then comes mess-gear— breakfast on the table. After breakfast he takes down towels, blackens shoes, and gets ready for quarters.

Colors at eight every morning, no matter when the sun rises. At nine, the bugle sounds the sick call; at half

The
Smoking-Lamp

past nine, quarters; muster, then drill. At eleven o'clock the bugle sounds retreat; and here is where you get in your extra work until noon, when the boatswain pipes: "To mess." Simultaneous with the piping, a red pennant is run up the yard-arm, where it floats for one hour. The meal pennant is always up at meal-times; and while it floats the smoking-lamp is lighted, and it is only when it is burning that smoking is allowed. The smoking hours are the meal hours, and during the evening recreation; though often, when there is no drill, nor other work it would interfere with, the officer-of-the-deck grants special permit for the lamp to burn. Dinner over, there are boxing, reading, and all sorts of things (including extra work) going on until half past one, when the bugle sounds "quarters." Then come instructions in gunnery, signals, seamanship, etc. Today I had boat-drill, pulling a 16- foot oar (not a bit like sculling for ducks).

After boat-drill we had to hoist and clean them, make up sails, and put fresh water into the breakers. There has been more scrubbing and cleaning, enough to keep us on the jump until after five, when we had fifteen minutes at "monkey-drill"—callisthenics; and were ready to answer the mess-pipe and sit down to supper at half past five. It is only then that the day's work is done: the smoking-lamp is left burning, boxing-gloves and punching-bags are brought on deck (Uncle Sam furnishes these as well as dumb-bells, Indian clubs, etc.), and joy revels uninterruptedly until, as the dusk gathers, you hear from the bridge the quartermaster announce to the officer-of-the-deck: "It is one minute to sundown, sir." The officer-of-the-deck tells the captain's orderly to tell the captain it is one minute to sundown. Returning from the captain's cabin, the orderly says: "The captain says, 'Make it so.'" The quartermaster, from the bridge, announces: "Sundown!" The officer of the deck says: "Sound it off." The drum gives three rolls, the bugle sounds colors—while every man on deck faces aft, stands at attention, and salutes the flag as it falls. At eight the bugle sounds "Hammocks." All hands stand in line, two by two, at the hammock netting. The boatswain's mate calls: "Uncover!" Hats are doffed, and a silence that lets in the sound of splashing water on the ship's sides settles over all as the chaplain comes on deck and offers a brief but fervent prayer for the loved ones at home and the sailors on the deep. Then: "Pipe down." All in less time than it takes to write it. Each hammock hangs on its own hooks. Some turn in at once, while others go on with the sport, or, as I am at this moment doing, write. At nine o'clock there comes the firing of guns and "Taps." If I can find the man who calls a sailor's life a lazy one, I should like to have a word with him.

Sunday, August 11th.

No matter what Sunday was intended to be, on a man-of-war it is verily not a day of rest. From the captain down, every one in authority is looking for trouble. They call it inspection, and once a month it is general muster. When I recall that there are fifty-two of them each year, and three years of them, I fear I shall be gray-headed before I am twenty-one years old.

Monday, August 12th.

Wrote a letter home tonight, so have no need to write here.

Tuesday, August 13th.

The routine work never changes; but sometimes it is one drill, and sometimes another. Today we had single-sticks—I always have liked fencing.

Wednesday, 14th.

Ought to get an answer tomorrow morning.

Thursday, 15th.

The letter came. It was short, but said, "Come home before you sail." I asked leave of the lieutenant commanding, and he tells me things which mean I'm "pledged" to Uncle Sam, and must put up "security" for my return. Have written the result of the interview home.

Friday, 16th.

While waiting an answer to last night's letter, will write the story of the bells.

Andy says I will disgrace my uniform if I do not stop talking about "getting up at five o'clock" instead of saying "turning out at two bells." On ship, there are as many hours in a day as there were blackbirds in the king's pie; but it takes twice that number of bells to tell their flight. Time, here, is divided into six watches of eight bells each, and each watch changes on eight bells. They are designated:

The Star Watch, which comes on at 8 bells. . . . . 4 A.M.
Morning Watch,   "   "   " " 8 bells . . . . 8 A.M.
Day Watch,   "   "   " " 8 bells . . . 12 noon
Dog Watch,   "   "   " " 8 bells . . . . . 4 P.M.
Farmer's Watch,   "   "   " " 8 bells . . . . . 8 P.M.
Graveyard Watch, "   "   " " 8 bells . . midnight
Star Watch,   "   "   " " 8 bells . . . . 4 A.M.
                                          1 bell . . . 4:30 A.M.
                                          2 bells { Reveille, 5 A.M.
                                          3 bells . . 5:30 A.M.
                                          4 bells . . . . 6 A.M.
                                          5 bells . . 6:30 A.M.
                                          6 bells . . . . 7 A.M.
                                          7 bells . . 7:30 A.M.
Day Watch,   "   "   " " 8 bells { Colors, 8 A.M.

Saturday, 17th.

Working like a dog, and waiting for my letter.

Sunday, August 18th.

Sunday and still waiting. I know it will be here in the morning.

Monday, August 19th.

Nine o'clock brought the letter, with twice the amount I need. Lieutenant commanding has granted me forty-eight hours leave, and I'm rushing for the 2:15 train.

Wednesday, August 21st.

Have washed off the slate and said good-by; and now let me whistle, "A life on the ocean wave."

Friday, 23rd.

Still coaling ship, and she looks like a raven. (So do I.)

Saturday, 24th.

We have scrubbed her fore and aft—she looks like a swan. (But I don't.)

San Francisco Bay, Sunday, August 25th.

Omitted much routine work in getting ready for sea. We have tested the patent life-preservers; those great, sugared doughnuts that hang at quarters, and found them fit. Should the cry come, "Man overboard!" immediately one will be dropped; the concussion

with the water will ignite a fuse, and instantly there will burn two lights upon it. The preserver is large enough to buoy up five or six men, and the lights on them will burn for twenty-four hours. It is understood that the man overboard is to make for the preserver. The life-boats are not to seek the man in the water, but to pull straight for the lights.

In the event of a collision, we know just where to find mats to stop the hole. And we know the fire-drill better than I know the wig-wag. If the call comes, "Abandon ship," we are ready. Today, into each boat, we put breakers of fresh water, a case of canned corned beef, and a case of hardtack. Hardtack for sea is put up in sealed tin boxes. Two of these are nailed inside a wooden case, which is then sewed up in canvas and painted. This makes a package about the size of a small trunk, and quite as natty looking. Each boat has its boat-box, which contains, among other things, a compass, sail needles and twine, a box of fish-hooks packed in tallow, etc. These are already in the boat, and each man—there are fourteen, including the officer, in the whale-boat I belong to—knows exactly where to go and what to bring. One will seize a mess-bucket, and throw into it a few plates, cups, spoons, etc. (each man has a knife always at the end of his lanyard); another gets more provisions; another a rifle; still another must bring two boxes of ammunition for it; someone gets out the oars, while others are at port to lower the boat. My task is to go to the officer's ward-room and bring the medical emergency box. I am not anticipating trouble; but should the order come, in eight minutes after the bugle sounds our many oars will dip water, and we will be pulling for life.

"Sailing, Sailing, over the Bounding Main."

Of course, the larders are stocked, and the refrigerators filled with fresh meat. The chests and other loose articles are lashed. We are all ready and with tomorrow's dawn the "Queen of the Pacific" will get under way.

Monday, August 26th. At sea.

At four bells, all in concert, the boatswains piped and called: "A-l-l hands on deck—u-p anchor!" Then the engines groaned, the propellers began their first earnest work, c-h-u-n-g—c-h-o-n-g went the machinery, and we were off. The pilot directed the man at the wheel; and the captain, in all his glory, stood on the bridge in the early morning watch.

It was five bells when we cleared the bar, and my heart beat time to the song in my brain:

Sailing, sailing, over the bounding main,
For many a stormy wind shall blow,
 Ere Jack comes home again.

There is a law of the sea that regulates the watch: If the ship sails on a date of even number, the port takes the first lookout; if it is on an odd date, the starboard. Being the twenty-eighth, the port took the watch at colors this morning. Every man in the crew from now on, while at sea, will be off and on duty, day and night, for four hours at a stretch, barring, of course, the break that comes in the dog-watch.

At sunset colors, the running lights come on; and while they burn there comes from the watchers on the bridge, with each succeeding bell, its announcement, thus: "eight bells, and a port bright light," "eight bells, and a starboard bright light." To this the masthead lookout answers back, "A-l-l's well!" And so on and on, through the watches of the night.

Cleaning, scrubbing, mess and quarter, all go on at sea just as in port.

As we came out of the Golden Gate this morning, we were met by a gentle zephyr, which grew and stiffened, until at noon it was a trade-wind that tonight is gathering for a storm.

Some of the boys are showing symptoms of *mal-de-mer*; fortunately, I have thus far escaped and, in consequence, have just been told that tonight I am to stand the first lookout in the graveyard watch.

At sea. Tuesday, August 27th.

When I tumbled out of my hammock at midnight, I was dumbfounded to find I could not keep my legs under me. I was thrown promiscuously about the gun-deck as I struggled to get into my clothes. I had but one thought, a wreck; and I expected every moment to hear the bugle sound, "Abandon ship!" But instead, the boatswain piped, "All hands on deck!" Together we put up steadying sails; then the port watch turned in, and we were on deck. I cannot recall just what was said as the watch was handed over to me; but I shall never forget that first night aloft. I clung like grim death to the shrouds, saw nothing, but answered, "All's well," to the bridge, as the dismal groaning of the rigging stole through my senses.

At sea, August 28th, Wednesday.

The storm has abated. My shipmates say I'm good for

twenty years in the navy. Was not sick during the storm, and took to the ratlines like a duck to water.

At sea, Thursday, August 29th.

The dog-watch was originally the dodge watch. It is as plain as day now: at sea the dog-watch, from eight bells, 4 PM, to eight bells, 8 PM, is cut at four bells, when the watch shifts, preventing the men from standing the same watch two consecutive nights; and it is at this shift the dog watch howls. It is the high jinks of the seaman. No longer does a challenge run, "I'll see you on shore"; but while the minstrel thrums his banjo, or rattles his bones; the wits crack jokes, and the old seaman spins his yarn; all scores are settled according to Queensbury rules, or by rough and tumble, as the contestants elect. Whichever it be, it is always a fair fight and no favor. Hurrah for the dog-watch!

BY THE BELL		BY THE CLOCK	
Eight	4	PM	
One	4:30	"	
Two	5	"	
Three	5:30	"	
SUPPER			
Four	6	"	
Five	6:30	"	
Six	7	"	
Seven	7:30	"	

August 30, Friday. At sea.

Ploughing the main; besides doing regular, as well as extra, duty on ship.

Saturday, August 31st.

The passing of the storm has left me so filled with good-will toward man that on the gun-deck this morning I greeted old McCue. He was not slow to acknowledge the salute, but he did it by telling me that "good-morning" is the kind of talk they use in young ladies seminaries. (One type of a man-of-war's-man.)

Sunday, September 1st.

Just like a ploughshare wakening the crickets in the stubble, the ship has all day startled the flying-fish. Apparently they sleep under the waves until wakened by the ship, when up they come. One of them, in its flight today, fell flopping on the forecastle, where I caught it in my hands. It was quite two feet long, and we had it for tonight's mess. The meat was sweet and delicious. I had been taught that flying-fish are from three to twelve inches in length; but this two-footer I saw with my own eyes and caught with my own hands.

All day we have been running races with great schools of porpoises. By thousands they run along with the ship, apparently playing leap-frog, like boys when school lets out.

Monday, September 2nd.

Will anchor at Honolulu tomorrow. Visions of tropical fruits picked fresh from their moorings go dancing through my brain—But I must not anticipate; this is only a place to register *what is.*

Tuesday, September 3, Honolulu.

Disgust and disappointment! My eyes were scarce

opened when I recognized Diamond Head. It is there, true enough, with its jagged cliffs and cocoanut-trees, just as you see it in the picture-books. But, as we came steering in, we were met by a tug whose mission was to report cholera in Honolulu; and here I am spending my first night in the tropics, not listening to native music, while I gorge myself with succulent fruits; but in quarantine, and still on sea-rations, with my clothes clinging to my body like adhesive plaster, and my lungs laboring in vain to be inflated with this slow, sultry, sweltering air.

September 4, Wednesday.

The uniform for each day is decided by the joint authority of the doctor and the commanding officer. One is actuated by climate and health, the other by the eternal fitness of things. Every ship carries a set of colored pictures of sailors in their various uniforms. They are laid loose in a frame measuring ten by twelve inches. Each day the one chosen is put next to the glass and hung on the log-writer's door; here goes the boatswain to get his cue, and while the men are breakfasting, pipes the order. Today it ran:

"The uniform for the day will be white working clothes, and bared feet."

I was breathing at every pore from excessive humidity, as I dragged myself to quarters—beginning to feel like an invalid, and feeling sure I should never smile again—when I cast a sidelong glance down the line, and grew faint from suppressed laughter. The feet of my shipmates were anything but in uniform. Some of them are so elaborately tattooed they look for all the world like carpet slippers; while others have only a star on each toe. Butterflies, either in sportive groups, or with one great sphinx-moth, covering the entire instep, are in high favor; while snakes and monkeys follow a close second. One fellow, an Irish-American, has one corner of the English

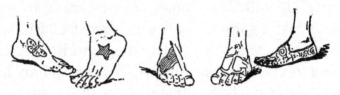

The shipmates' feet.

flag running up the side of his ankle, the main part being where he ever tramples upon it. I judge that it is only after a second enlistment that the tattoo fever gets into one's feet. Personally, I think I can serve my whole term without its attacking any part of my anatomy.

Thursday, September 5th.

Although the routine of ship life is so monotonous that one might think to keep its record by writing dates and ditto, when night comes we always find it different from yesterday. Today the cleaning of the smoking-lamp fell to my lot. The smoking-lamp is shaped like a conductor's lantern, with a great tray at the bottom, like the brass relics of our ancestors. It is made with open sides and unglazed; within its bright frame a lard-oil lamp burns, but not always—only at prescribed hours: at meal hours, the dog-watch, and by the gracious leave of the deck officer, but never when the magazines are open. It always hangs on the gun-deck with a tub of water beneath it—a damp sepulcher for burnt-offerings.

Sunday, September 8th.

With heat and discontent, this log is narrowing to bi-weekly records; but I must not overlook the native fishermen. Their craft is a light canoe, made seaworthy by bamboo outriggers extending four or five feet over its sides. These boats carry from two to four men, who make a pleasing picture with their black bodies scantily clad in weathered white. We are anchored about a mile from the surf. The fishes have made our backyard their camping ground, and here the fishermen come with their nets, shaped like huge chain purses made from twine. The clasp is of bamboo, and when set has an opening of from ten to twelve feet; a little bag lying at the bottom is jerked open, causing the bait to float. The moment it starts, schools of little fish dart above it; the clasp is sprung, the net hauled into the boat, emptied, and reset. I fancy that on shore they cook the fish; but here, just as one enjoys a cherry when picking, they daintily take the head between their thumb and finger, put the rest into their mouth, and eat it with a gusto that makes us wish for a small-fry. The doctor says all the fish have cholera; so we are still eating "salt-horse" and cursing our fate.

It was this very fate that drove Timmy, an apprentice, to go fishing one night off Honolulu. Now for a man-of-war's-man to drop a fishing line over the side would be no less a crime than the spiking of a turret-gun; but there are ways unknown to the powers that rule, and it was for Timmy to embrace one. The foot of Tim's hammock peeps through a porthole on the berth-deck, and here he set his baited hook and waited for a nibble. In this stifling climate time loses its reckoning—it seems interminable. Sleep lured, and a craving stomach pleaded. Tim compromised by turning ends, and, fastening the line about his great toe, yielded to sweet slumber. How long he slept does not matter, but the yell that rent that night-watch will never be forgotten. They who ran to the rescue found him clinging to his hammock clews, his eyes starting from their sockets, yelling like an Indian, "Glory! I've lost a leg!" A shipmate, hastening above, reached over, and, cutting the line from the all but severed toe, landed a magnificent fish. We called it a sixty-pounder, though it was never weighed. It seemed a cross between a salmon and a perch. It was smuggled in and distributed to its limit, proving delicious eating, and the only decent meal we have had in Hawaii.

Tim's fish.

Chapter II

Rolling Off The Log

A log is a thing you have to write on every day you live, or it ceases to be a log. See what a mess I have made of it! But the old saw, "There is nothing easier than rolling off a log," shows me my way out. I am just going to roll off the log right here on the spot, and write impressions and reminiscences just as they occur to me.

We are anchored about a mile out from the surf, seemingly as motionless as "a painted ship upon a painted ocean," while the shifting panorama of Molokai shows us to be riding great ground-swells.

When on top we see the leper villages, guarded by sharp rocks cutting the waves as they ride shoreward, and tossing the spray fifty or a hundred feet into the air, whence it falls into a snowy foam, like a garland of white roses upon a living sepulcher. The swell goes on, and the blue, blue ocean cuts away the shore-line, leaving to our vision only the far-reaching, towering cliffs with their tropical verdure and purple ravines; and thus, come again, go again, shifts the picture; while the waves that splash the sides of the ship whisper "Unclean."

I blush to own it, but I so longed for a closer look that I was delighted to be of a cutter-crew which carried the American consul from our ship, out to meet the little white leper ship. She is a small steamer that plies among the islands, picking up the unfortunate, and carrying them to this place of refuge. As we drew alongside, the consul boarding her upper deck, I could look in on the lower. She is fitted with seats, back-to-back, like those on the Oakland ferry. There were about twenty victims that day. Some of them were in irons, and swearing like pirates. There were but two women; they clung about each other's neck and cried piteously. There was nothing in their appearance suggestive to me of anything worse than an advanced stage of consumption, or "dope fiend." We were not there longer than half an hour; and, in shoving away from her, I noticed every one used oar or boat-hook, instead of placing hands upon the leper-boat.

At another time it was in a whale-boat that took our doctor ashore to visit the settlement. It is a rough landing at all times, sometimes impossible to make; but with tide and wind in our favor, we easily made it. Our doctor was met at the landing and taken to the village. While awaiting his return, I noticed men going about attending to their duties in the most ordinary manner, and it was only when I observed the two guards we had brought along, standing with loaded guns and bayonets, I remembered that on three occasions the lepers had taken boats away from visitors, and made their escape. I then realized that the men with the guns were not bits of red tape, but a wisely ordained means of precaution.

While we waited, I thought of many things, and was sadly glad when we gave way on our oars and pulled for the *Olympia*.

If there is a day on board that a sailor can call his own, it is Rope-Yarn Sunday, which always falls on Wednesday. It is then he mends or puts his traps in shipshape. What an odd picture the deck presented today! Half a dozen little hurdy-gurdy sewing-machines running, some cobbling, and all sorts of things which a fellow used to have done he must do for himself. It is a good chance, when time permits, to write a letter home, and I noticed an old sailor: he had written U.S.F.S., when off came his cap, and, while he held it in his left hand, scanning the band, he slowly wrote "*Olympia.*" He wears half a dozen enlistment stripes on his arm, and whether he had, for the moment, forgotten what ship he was on, or whether it was a lesson in orthography he was studying, no one dared ask.

It has been said that the native of India rejoices not more over the killing of a tiger than the native Hawaiian over the killing of a tiger-shark. Sharks are so numerous about ships that it has ceased to be a novelty to hook either the dog or mackerel species–ranging in length from four to eight feet—and dispatch it with a battle-ax. But, yesterday, an officer shot a tiger, or basking-shark, that must have measured more than thirty feet in length. It was wounded and bleeding, when the men from the fishing-boats saw it, and begged that it be not shot again, but given to them. These sharks, though more than three times the size, are not so dangerous as some of the smaller species. They made fast to it and towed it into the surf, where some swimmers started a gladsome sound, which was taken up, repeated again and again, until a veritable song of rejoicing ensued, which wakened the

The Olympia.

sleepers on the beach. In a twinkling, the white surf was alive with black bodies. They came into the water, bringing clubs and knives. They fairly fought each other for points of vantage. They clubbed and cut, rode on its back, and beat it with their feet and fists, until resistance ceased; then the multitude hauled it upon the beach, where some spent the excess of their fury by throwing themselves upon the creature and imbedding their teeth in the carcass.

It was a scene of interest to us landlubbers, but Seaman McCue says, "Sharks ain't no more than sunfish to a man with any sort o' nerve. Why, back in the early seventies, when I was here in these very waters, me and a shipmate was in swimmin', when a big man-eater planted his teeth right in my left thigh. I hadn't no knife, of course, and I gin him a hit with my fist, but his d— old hide was so tough he never felt it, but was swimming out with me fast. I seen my shipmate pulling for shore, and I knowed I couldn't wait for orders, so I just turned and bit my teeth in his old jaw (I've got awful powerful jaws myself), and the way that shark opened his'n and sailed for the deep seas was a caution. Pshaw! them Kanacky darkies is showin' off, that's all."

The call to general quarters, or battle-drill, we answer as readily as the mess-call. Although it has no stated time, and is supposed to come as a surprise, whether in port or at sea it has always come in the daytime. But last week, when we were anchored well out at sea, our object being to test compass, etc., it was 2-bells before the mid-watch—"in his hammock at midnight the sailor boy lay"—when the gongs sounded "Cast loose and provide."

It was the battle-call! In less time than it takes to write it, every officer, every man, was at his station: beside the guns, at the magazine, at the ammunition-hoists, or in the torpedo room. Then as, in waking from sleep, a giant monster strains each separate muscle until its whole being is alert with action, so each man does his part. Up the hoists come the ammunition, cartridges weighing from one pound to those weighing two hundred and fifty being handled with equal facility. The guns are loaded. The next order is, "Aim!" followed ordinarily by "Secure!" Then the loads are withdrawn, returned to the magazines, and the drill is over. But that night, instead of "Secure," the bugle sounded "Fire!" Not a man blundered, but I am sure the stars in heaven ceased to twinkle, as twenty-three guns went off in unison. Was the order given to test us, or was a junior officer giving orders in his dreams? We shall never know.

Hawaii, "the Paradise of the Pacific," whose praises men never cease to sing, has been to us anything but a Paradise for six long, murky, sultry weeks. The imps of Hades have been in the air. Our navigator was sunstruck, and was sent home the second week we were here. Even the volcano has sulked, and not a glimmer of his lurid splendor has he flaunted for us. And all the time we have been without fresh meat; eating yams—the Almighty certainly intended them for firewood, and not for Christian stomachs—and not a lemon or a lime to brew a cooling drink. Even our first mail was destroyed in the precautionary fumigation. If ever we come closer to mutinying, I shall hope not to be there. With rations unfit and insufficient, we felt like prisoners in a workhouse, and we acted the part. Coal was unnecessarily wasted by spilling into the sea; men sulked, and refused to work. When they were put into the brig, their shipmates called: "Let them out, or put us in, too." And I believe there wasn't a mother's son of us who would not have been glad to jump ship and swim home had it been possible. Oh, it is a bitter dose this, but I poured it out myself, and am going to keep swallowing and never squeal.

Matters were growing from bad to worse, when, finally, being reduced to neither salt nor pepper, we called for the skipper. Like a father he came to us, asking, "What is it, my boys?" Once our troubles were laid before him, everything changed.

Captain Reed is a man and an officer, every inch of him, and he has a crew that will stand by him until the ocean freezes over.

CHAPTER III

A TYPHOON

The lingering sun seemed listening to the sweet strains of "Aloha" as they floated out from the shore; the captain had said it was sunset; the boatswain piped "A-l-l–ll hands u-p anchor!" and we bade a fond, a glad farewell to Hawaii as our running lights came on.

In this little, new world afloat I have been learning so many things that I had not noticed our lights, but, missing one from half way up the mainmast rigging, I asked Andy what had be come of it.

I think I detected a tinge of disgust in his voice when he asked me if I had never heard of an anchor light burning at sea. Then he showed me how all of the electric lights were placed where their beams would fall entirely within the ship. With the exception of the running lights (four in all) we were, to the man in the moon, in darkness. On either end of the bridge a triangular box, or reflector, holds a light: the starboard end a green, the port a red. At the stern of the ship, and directly in its middle, a white light is boxed, while from the foretop a white, bright light that rivals Sirius, the dog-star, proclaims over the whole world of waters that she is a man-of-war.

During the night we passed numberless islands, but

by noon on the following day there was no land in sight, and though the feel of the tropics lingered in our bones, the keen breath of old Ocean soon drove us into watch-caps and jerseys. Neptune was sleeping. His long-drawn breathing waved his blue blanket into billows whose only gleam of white was a feathery froth cut by our ship and trailed in our wake, and into whose spray the tiny storm-petrels hung their slender legs, apparently treading the water, which was growing dark and darker, frowning back at the darkening sky above.

Old salts will tell you that Mother Carey controls her chicks as unfailingly as the barometer controls its mercury, but it was the latter the officers depended upon; and whenever a chance could be found we would hasten 'midship, hoping against reason, but the tell-tale silver was sinking, sinking, in the barometer. Steadying sails were hoisted, the guns trained in, life-boats made ready in their cradles with their oars doubly lashed. In short, we "secured" for a storm, and were scarce ready when an ugly green sea rushed upon us, pouring brine into every corner of the ship.

Because Bill Phelan discovered a cozy corner on the gun-deck where men could lie and snooze when off duty, it was, even before we left San Francisco, christened the "Phelan Building." When this particular sea went over us, it left six inches of water on the gun-deck, and the boys crawled out, declaring the Phelan Building was swamped. Bill never stirred. The ship rose and pitched, while the spent water rushed fore and aft with the force of a hydraulic monitor, and still Bill hung to a stanchion, apparently unruffled. When his shipmates pleaded with him to come along, he answered by asking:

"Do you think I am going to leave all this nice warm water to go out in the cold storm? Don't disturb me, please, until the smoke-stacks are under."

But a treble from the bos'n's pipe summoned all hands on deck, for there was an alarming odor permeating the whole ship. There was a regular search party set on the track of those fumes. Day and night it never abated, and after forty-eight hours search, a fire was reported in a coal-bunker situated in dangerous proximity to the aft 8-inch magazine. It was unquestionably a case of spontaneous combustion. The coal, evidently being damp, had ignited under the friction caused by the ship's roll; but it was not the *cause* that interested us now, it was the threat and how to avert it.

To have done our fire-drill would have proved disastrous; instead, then, of turning the hose with salt water into the bunkers, the hollow compartment surrounding the ammunition magazine was flooded, and the black-gang, like rats in a grain-bin, dug into the coal; and while they fought the fire below, a perfect discipline reigned on deck: hatches and gun- and air-ports were doubly secured; life-lines we rove from rail to stanchions; crossing and recrossing, knotting and tying, we wove a network over and about the whole ship. Along her sides we trailed oil-bags, and the sea-anchor, a great, bulky parachute, was cast astern, where it dragged and sulked like a bulldog at its chain, while the grinding waters on the ship's sides sounded not unlike his growl, and the ship stood on beam ends, while mountainous billows rode under her; or she stood trembling in every fiber, gathering strength for the onset, and she would cut through the sea like a torpedo shot from its gun. Then she would rock and roll, her masts whipping the brine like fly-rods on a trout-stream.

Releasing hold of the life-line for one instant as he was going inside, a man was dashed piteously, and stunned, against the turret. Before he could recover himself, the returning wash bore him away with as little ado as if at drill. The life-buoy was loosened from its trigger, and the order was trumpeted to "Man the life-boat."

Whale-boat No. 22, hanging at the lee, was called away. We were all, twelve men and a coxswain, in place ready to cast adrift, when the skipper, who had no sense but sight left, trumpeted from the bridge, "Belay that life-boat."

I stopped praying, and thanked God.

When the men down there below got the fire under control it broke out in two more bunkers; then there were no longer black-gang nor deck-hands. Everybody (even the marines, who never work) took a turn. At first we shoveled the burning coal into sacks, dragging it to the fire-room; but the sacks would burn away, spilling their fiery contents before we could reach the furnace. Thus we were forced to keep to the iron buckets. One man at a time would crawl through a small door into the smoldering bunkers, shovel a bucketful, and hasten away to make room for the next. We dared not throw one shovelful over board, for it was our fuel, the ship's only hope.

The iron walls of the engine-room caught one stray note from the rhapsody of the storm, and held it in a tremolo that silenced the hissing voices of flaming tongues licking in the smoldering coals; and in their fantastic wavings I saw, in memory, a little child dip the

The captain in oilskins.

"Life-lines we rove from rail to stanchions."

"At first we shoveled the burning coal into sacks."

pretty tips of a long peacock-feather brush into a burning grate, lift it proudly above his head, and march away with his flamboyant torch in his left hand, while his right beat an imaginary drum, and his baby lips toot-toot-tooted an air that marked his "marching through Georgia."

It was a strange time and place to recall such a scene in my babyhood, but I remembered still further they had said I was truly doomed to some fearful ending, and I was wondering if it had not come, when another sea broke above, and drove us under tons of water down into the deep.

For nine days the fires continued, sometimes smoldering, sometimes raging just like the typhoon that played with the ship, and during those nine days and nights, which seemed like ninety, there was neither hammock nor mess. Hardtack and coffee, taken as one could catch it, was the only ration.

Human endurance has its limit.

The gases became so overpowering below that many succumbed and had to be hoisted to the deck to be resuscitated by the breath of the storm. It became necessary to number us into line, that none might shirk, checking us off as our turn came to shovel a bucketful and hasten to the air. Officers and men, all begrimed into a common blackness, would fall exhausted upon the decks, to sleep until roused to fresh action. Sometimes the sky would become overcast and day seem like night; then the blessed rain would come in torrents that quelled the waves; but the clouds would ride on, and the wind and the waves, as if mad to have been checked, would redouble their fury, and we always faced the storm. The little wheel in the chart-house, by which one man under the direction of an officer can steer in an ordinary sea, took four, tugging with their might, to handle.

The captain, who was omnipresent, seemed always there, eyes fixed on the binnacle, signaling orders that could not be heard. Then Quartermaster Swift would leave his side, and, with his lantern tucked inside his coat, struggle forth to hold the reel, often returning to report that instead of making two hundred miles a day, more than one day we made not a single mile.

It was not a wash of waves. Great, ugly, green seas would pile up and stand like mountains. Then the demon Wind, with a cutlass between his teeth, would cut the crest clean away, and hurl tons upon tons of water upon us; and when their repeated assaults were loosening the anchor clamps on the cat-heads, we were obliged to go with rope lashings to doubly secure them. In doing this we lay at times buried under tons of water, and when we came out we could not speak for the noise of the tempest.

While all this was going on we were given extra instruction in the order to "Abandon ship." Each division comprises forty-four men and two officers, divided into two watches. Lieutenant Sherman and Midshipman Todd

The *Olympia* in a typhoon. "I saw only the surging, seething waters, engulfing the decks."

were in charge of my division, and they went from man to man, screaming their orders into our ears. We already knew our places and what to do, but the general plan for the emergency was explained again to each. Should the moment arrive when the fires could no longer be controlled, we were to go as a fleet.

We have launches, boats, dingys, and catamarans sufficient to carry every man in the crew. The sailing-launch with its tall masts to carry signals, would have taken the lead as flag-ship. She was already equipped with charts, one to be given to the officer of each of the other boats, that in the event of their being buffeted apart in the sea, each craft, with the aid of chart and compass, might make its own way to Silver Island. After the last boat should have cast loose, Captain Reed, with the lead-bound book under his arm, would enter his gig with its golden arrow, and shoot out for the new flag-ship, of which he would be the admiral.

The captain, in a typhoon, is not the gilded idol that stands upon the bridge on entering port. Begrimed with soot he is incased in oilskins and a sou'wester that cannot keep out the damp, and he is no better to look upon than an old salt on a whaler.

On the tenth day, when the storm was spent and the sea was like oil, when the fires were quenched and the ship was running her prescribed knots, the captain called us to muster. Stanchions and railings lay like twisted straws along the decks, the chart-house was stove in and partly washed away, the paint was battered from our sides, and red rust mingled with black soot to disfigure her still further; but it was not to review these things he called us: it was to express his sorrow at the loss of one of his crew, and his pride at the willingness every man had shown when the life-boat was called. He explained touchingly and briefly that he could not sacrifice thirteen men, for he realized that it was hopeless to go after him when we were every moment shipping seas.

How I wish I could write something that would convey just an idea of a typhoon—what it was like, and how we felt. Four hundred and forty-four human lives were imperiled and not a man whimpered.

From fighting the fire, we would joyously go for a trick at the wheel, and although it was a tug that called for strength nearly superhuman, the wind that cut our breath away was freighted with noxious vapors.

O night, and storm and darkness, ye are wondrous
    strong,
        Yet lovely in your strength—

for you can pin men to the mast, and let them sleep. I recall a night so dark that the darkness could almost be felt. The frenzied wind blowing off the crests of black seas was hurling them hundreds of feet ahead of the break, and they stung me with biting brine as I stood in the foretop listening for the stroke of the bell. My ear was glued to the speaking-tube, yet the shout that was sent up from the bridge came to me in the faintest of whispers: "What's the matter aloft?" and though I could not hear my own voice I screamed back, "Can't hear the bell, sir; a-l-l-l-'s well!"

Oh, the winds, the winds, the winds! Who can tell their story?

Again, I stood on the signal yards, but it was day. They screamed and roared, and yelled, drowning every other sound. Like boys creating new noises by breathing across the mouths of empty bottles, they cut across the smoke-stacks and moaned into their cavernous tubes. Then, exhausted by their own fury, they flagged and soughed through the rigging, quickening every line and ratline into a wh-h-r-r-rr- and a Rr-r-r-r-ra-rattling that swelled into melody such as no æolian harp has ever played before; then, blending into a single note, a deep monotone struck masts and yards, rising and falling, rising and falling, like the blue ocean in a calm.

It brought balm to my weariness, and, looking down the slim mast, I discovered that the ship was gone; I saw only the rushing, surging, seething waters engulfing the decks, and from my exalted height I felt like a bird of the greenwood blown out to sea.

Lieutenant Buchanan told me one night, when we were buffeted against one another on the bridge, that I would never meet another blow like this, and men are wondering how the ship ever lived it through, but I think I know.

The flag-ship is a thing alive. It has its parts and being. We have heard it breathe, and who will question that in Captain Reed it has both brain and soul?

Who has not watched the Reaper shake his sickle in men's faces, when many would lie down and die, while one, like a panther at bay, would fight him off and live on?

That is why, like a stormy-petrel, the *Olympia* rode through the typhoon.

CHAPTER IV

I t was on a Sunday morning in early November we cast anchor in beautiful Tokyo Bay, so written of by traveler and sketched by artist, that it was like an old, familiar scene. The white sails of the mackerel fleet speckle the water like polka-dots on a blue necktie. Fuji Yama stands a majestic background to the whole picture, while from the American consulate Old Glory floats with a majesty and beauty I never before recognized in his brilliant folds. It was a sight that brought my heart to my throat, for I felt—words can never tell that feeling, but it comes to every one the first time he finds himself in an alien land.

But a sampan, with six half-nude figures all standing sculling with long oars, was bringing our mail, and I fancied their stroke on the smooth water was playing a song my grandmother used to sing as she worked among the flowers in her conservatory at home:

Good news from home, good news for me,
Has come across the deep, blue sea,
From friends that I have left in tears,
From friends that I'll not see for years.

I improvised, and, hastening to the deck, received my letters, while in silence the old song sung itself out,

For now the joyful hour has come,
That I have heard good news from home.

Whether Sunday comes at sea or in port, it makes no difference. After Quarters the bell solemnly tolls, as the master-at-arms calls, "Keep silence above the decks during Divine Service." Then the church pennant is run up the foremast, and the sky-pilot brings his little table out on the starboard side of the gun-deck. Attendance is not compulsory. The captain generally is in evidence; and just enough other officers to set an example for the men, occupy chairs along the sides, while four mess benches are quite sufficient to seat the rest of the congregation. The sermon is never long, and for music, "Anchored" and other songs of the sea are interspersed with good old Methodist hymns, and are sung in or out of tune to the accompaniment of mandolin and guitar.

Apropos of the importance of the captain being present at Divine Service, a reminiscence relates how a captain being late one morning, the chaplain (an Episcopalian) after waiting for what he considered a reasonable length of time, began in an ecclesiastical voice, "The Lord is in His holy temple," when suddenly the cabin door flew open and the captain, half uniformed, his face a mirror of indignation, yelled, "*Sky-pilot ahoy!* I want you to distinctly understand the Lord is *not* in His holy temple until I am seated."

During church hour the lamp burns, but smoking is restricted to the spar-deck and forecastle.

When we left Hawaii, every last mother's son of us was in the fourth conduct class; but after the fire the captain wiped off the slate and put us all in the first class.

Ship conduct is rated in classes. There are:

A Star Class: That means anything you ask for; but you have to grow wings before you can get into it.

First Class entitles you to draw all your pay every month, and to enjoy all the shore-leave your watch is entitled to.

The Second Class draw half-pay, and are restricted to the ship for twenty-two days.

The Third Class get shore-leave only every forty-five days and draw one third their pay.

The Fourth Class means on the ship for three months with only one quarter of your pay, which barely covers mess money and tobacco. Every man on ship must go ashore at least once in three months.

When you have served your time in the fourth class, you do not jump to the first, but, by slow degrees, back through the intervening classes; thus, if ever you get back to Class One, you will have spent 157 days in accomplishing it.

To get "in the brig" drops you from any place into the fourth class.

Arriving on the third (a date with an odd number) gave the starboard watch first leave. That meant me, and seventy-two hours on terra-firma!

Landed at the English hettaba. Walking up the steps and through the custom-house yard unquestioned, we found 'rickshaws as numerous as boats in the bay; and need I note we each got into one? Hastening to the exchange, we doubled our coin, and proceeded without delay, to "do" Japan. The first day we stuck to the baby carts, completely surrendering ourselves to the little, brown, two-legged human horses, who, without questioning us, probably out of deference to our uniform, landed us at the Travelers Rest. I do not think Baedeker makes mention of it, neither would I, only it is entitled to some notice, being the first stopping-place in Yokohama. The building is of semi-European construction, whose interior decoration is not of fans and lanterns, but of ship models and flags, interspersed with gay-colored pictures of Jap geisha-girls. The one in question is kept by Mickey O' Herron, an ex-man-o'-war's-man, who deals out drinks, both soft and hard, to the sea-worn wanderers of all nations.

Travelers' rest.

While at the Rest, some of the men grew so very fond of their rickshaw runners that they repeatedly drank to their good health, and glutted them with American beverages, until, when the day was ending, there was to be seen in the streets more than one sailor uniform standing in the shafts, while an unconscious Jap lolled on the cushions of the jinrikishas.

Among the number who went ashore that day was

the ship's cook. I recognized him at midnight, as we came from the Benton Dora. He lay curled up like a coil of gear, beside a feeble charcoal-fire, underneath a shelter of matting, sleeping with the rickshaw runners. There was nothing new to him in port; and every man to his own fancy for enjoyment. But this is the sequel: instead of returning to the ship on Friday noon, with the rest of the fellows, he came out in a sampan some time in the night, and, as is his wont on such occasions, went to the galley and made for himself a sandwich from canned corned beef and dry English mustard. The next morning, when his assistant went into the galley and would have

Lolling in the jinrikishas.

removed the remnants of the repast, he discovered that, in lieu of mustard, the cook had eaten Rough-on-Rats. Without giving the alarm, he hastened that he might be the first at the hammock of his dead chief, but found him peacefully snoring. Today he is at his post again.

The Benton Dora of Yokohama is the only part of the town that has escaped European influence. The sights one sees here have been so often and so well described that I may omit them; but after my first day ashore, with head aching from the incessant rasping ting-a-ling they call music, I sought the barracks of the Salvation Army. And right here is a fine place for me to write my first eulogy.

At home I had often heard that the Salvation Army was doing good work, but I had never so much as given it a thought. The branch here comes from England, and the lassies wear a gray uniform, which, coupled with their quiet, winsome manner, gives them something of the appearance of an order of nuns. There is neither drum, tambourine, nor gospel hymns at the barracks; just nice, clean, warm dormitories with "comfy" white beds, where, for a reasonable remuneration, one may secure a decent lodging. For this every man in the navy should take off his hat. Next morning, as we came out, there were our 'rickshaws of the previous day, each runner claiming his own. We kept them for a while, but it seemed so inhuman for those toy men to be trundling great, husky Americans about that we dismissed them, and hired bicycles. I wish I were a writer. I would begin a book today and call it "Wheeling Through Japan"; there would be nothing original in the title, but the cover-plate at least would be unique, just a man dressed in sailor uniform, on a wheel. I have seen it.

Bicycling in Yokohama.

Our seventy-two hours up, we were back betimes, and the port watch went on shore.

It is so cold that the mustering uniform calls for pea-jackets. The change from the Islands here was very marked; but I think the boys of the Pacific Coast are standing the weather better than those from Nebraska, who have been cradled in snow-drifts. In the bay, as on shore, it seems to be one continual play-day. The cheapness of laundering, and the facilities for bringing and taking, have made wash-day on shipboard a thing of the past; while the dirtiest job we ever had to perform, coaling, has become the very poetry of the sea, in which the prosy Jackies take no part. Alongside come bulky lighters with their black freight; in the sampans follow men and women, all in blue and white, with their heads turbaned. They form themselves into a living chain, extending from the lighters to the bunker chutes. The men shovel the coal into pretty grass baskets, that look as though they were woven for the holding of spring blossoms. Each basket will contain about a shovelful. When filled, a woman picks it up, tosses it to the next, who in turn tosses it up and on, their arms moving in perfect rhythm to the song they chant; and so quickly do they perform the task, it seems like magic. I stood in admiration watching them, thinking how very sweet sounded their song, for it is unaccompanied by the samisen, when Lieutenant Sturdy roused me from my reverie by asking how much of the wigwag I knew. When I answered that I did not know, he proceeded to find out; and when it proved to be only seven letters, he set me to learn the other nineteen. The result? With a red flag bearing a white square in its center on sunny days, or with the colors reversed on cloudy, I can communicate as far as the flag can be seen with any United States man-o'-war's-man, just as simply as I used to hold up two fingers, signaling across the school-room that I wanted someone to go swimming with me.

Just as the port watch was returning from its seventy-two hours' leave, two of our guns were fired. I asked Andy why they saluted the port on return, and not us? He pointed toward the Bund and at the signal on the Homoka lightship, and told me they had sighted an American mail, and that it was up to us to proclaim it to all Americans in Yokohama.

"Another mail!" It made me so happy that I walked to the rail and began whistling, "Two Little Girls in Blue"; but before I had finished the second line, the officer-of-the-deck came up and told me that the bo's'n could do all the whistling that was required on the ship, and that my services could be dispensed with.

Whew! it was the first moment I had ever felt like whistling since that day I went to attend a battle of roses in Santa Cruz; saw, for the first time, a ship for battle— fell in love with her, ran away, giving up everything in the world to go with her. There had been so much to learn I had not noticed that no one whistled, and I asked Andy why, in the slang of the ship, he had not "put me wise." He answered that old Mac's recipe was worth remembering: "Youngster, don't do nothing what's comfortable on board ship, it's agin' orders."

There is a sequel to my whistle. When silenced, I merely stood looking into the bay. The officer could not stand that, so he asked:

"What are you doing?"

"Nothing, sir."

"Nothing?"

"No, sir."

"Nothing at all?"

"No, sir."

"Work all done?"

"Yes, sir."

"Bright work shined?"

"Yes, sir."

"Well, well, well, this is a sad state of affairs: a man-o'-war's-man with nothing to do. Count the sails on the bay, and, when you get through, come and report to me how many there are."

Grumbling under my breath, I stood looking over the hammock netting. Finally I saw the mail-boat coming; I caught the rhythm of the oars and applied it to my turbulent spirits, and just as the sampan came alongside, I walked, deferentially, up to the officer-of-the-deck, saluted him, and said:

"There are seven thousand and eleven, sir."

He could not question the statement for neither he, nor any other man living could any more count those sails than he could count the stars in the Milky Way.

Familiar as the picture has become, it always amuses me each noon to see the officer-of-the-deck officially "fed." The ship's cook, in a white blouse, carrying a bowl of soup in one hand, and a plate with a sample of meat in the other, comes on deck and presents it to him; sometimes he only tastes, but in the colder climate the bowl is generally drained. This is by no means the officer's dinner, but one of his duties; he must each day know that the soup and meat are up to the standard.

The great, beautiful, landlocked Yedo Bay, with its magnificent fortifications right in the channel, seemed as secure a harbor as one could well imagine; but when we steamed twelve miles south and saw no sign of a dry-dock, but turning landward made straight for the bluffs, I felt that a catastrophe was imminent. However, to my astonished delight, the cliff opened and we rode into Yokosuka Bay, an inlet from Yedo. It is not only landlocked, but it is cliff-bound, surrounded and hemmed in by mountains that slope back from the water, forming an ideal amphitheater, with an area of more than seven thousand acres surrounding the bay. Here are the shipyards, arsenals, and magazines of Japan's navy. The bay is dotted all about with islands, every one of which that commands a fire is equipped with an up-to-date battery; the others with magazines or barracks. Inside the bay, we were met by a messenger who directed us to an empty magazine, that was at our disposal.

Anchoring about a mile out from the docks—there are three of them, magnificent stone affairs,—we unloaded all of our ammunition, packing it on lighters and towing it to safety. The Japs have not suspected us for disguised Chinese, but should a jar set off our explosives during repairs, it would be good-by to their docks, and death to many a sailor.

The Japanese sailor is by far the largest type of their countrymen I have seen. Their uniform is identical with that of the English navy, the only difference being the lettering on the cap-bands. (What mushy little caps they are, too, compared with our jaunty flat-tops!)

The excess of work over play here has threatened to "make Jack a dull boy."

Here are temples, shrines, and banners intermingled with war paraphernalia; but the most interesting sight to me is a Chinese battleship that was sunk by the Japs in the battle of the Yalu, in Korea Bay. This splendid naval battle has gone down into history; but it will not be told

Fuji Yama, the sacred mountain of Japan.

Shoveling snow from the turret roof.

that the *Ching Yuen,* which was sunk with others, has been raised and brought here as a souvenir of what can be done in five hours' fighting. I have been all through her. Inside she was painted white, and the walls of the torpedo room, where sixty Chinese were killed by a Japanese shell, is a veritable slaughter house, where the blood of the victims bespatter the walls and encrust the floor—a ghastly record of a glorious victory. But it is its exterior that first attracts: still in its war paint, a sort of bluish drab, or drabbish blue, every hole, scratch, or dent, put there by the victors, has been outlined with a broad streak of white paint.

We have been here in the dry-dock for two weeks, and today are as spick-and-span as on the morning we sailed away from San Francisco. Tomorrow we go back to anchor in Yokohama Harbor, and there will be nothing there, neither Jap, French, German, English, nor of any other nation, that can hold a candle alongside of us— white as the snow on Fuji-yama, with colors flying from our stern, the pennant streaming from the main truck, and the union jack on our bow—it never flies at sea, and in port only when everything is shipshape. Surely, never went a bride more radiantly to meet her spouse at the altar than we are going to meet our rear-admiral. As soon as we are anchored, the band from the *Baltimore* will come to us, and with it, new life. Colors, even, will take on new formality. In the morning the strains of "The Star Spangled Banner" will accompany the breaking of the flag, while at sunset it will be "Hail, Columbia."

Chapter V

Snow—The Baltimore—A Rear-Admiral—New Year's Day

All night long, unceasingly, in feathery flakes the snow had fallen. At daybreak I should have thought the magic of the night had transplanted us to the Arctic, only there was the undeniable outline of the sacred mountain. It seemed that the old volcano had belched in the night, for the white of his crest had run down over his sides, even to the water edge; while on the shore not a red tile remained. The steps of the hettabas and the roofs of our turrets were alike upholstered in ermine. From sky to sea it was one great, undulating drift of snow. Specks of emerald breaking through, told where the dwarf pines were buried, while streaks of crimson and gold pricked out the outline of temple and towers. I had never thought to realize the beauty of Bret Harte's snow picture in "The Outcasts of Poker Flat." *I cannot write about it;* but I have seen snow.

The crisp air is invigorating; but the shoveling of snow from the decks has a tendency to take the poetry out of things, and I am bothered about the poor naked devils who live on the water. How is a handful of charcoal burning in a teacup going to keep them from freezing to death?

"When Music, heavenly maid, was young," she took

61

no more joy into early Greece than the brass band that came with other belongings of a flagship, to us from the *Baltimore*. It plays twice a day, and in the evening it is a full orchestra, to whose strains we while away the dog-watch in waltz, hornpipe, or cake-walk, as the tune invites.

Last Thursday, November 28, was Thanksgiving; we had turkey on board, and behaved like the Americans that we are.

Yesterday, the *Baltimore* signaled to us for permission to get under way. Granted, the bo's'n piped, "A-l-l h-a-n-d-s on deck to cheer ship!" From the captain and the bandmaster, down we came. The Jackies on both ships stood on the rails or went into the rigging. From the main truck of the *Baltimore* streamed a "homeward-bounder." It is a pennant two hundred and fifty feet long. At its tip a bladder is attached to keep it afloat when it dips to the sea. The homeward-bounder has its superstitions too sacred to write; but it is the talisman that will carry the ship through wind and storm, until "Safe, safe, at last, the harbor passed," she will anchor in San Francisco Bay.

I do not quite retain the picture; for "Auld Lang Syne" from the quarter-deck sounded so startlingly new to me that everything else became subdued to my wondering where and when I had ever heard it before. But my memory could muster nothing but my first night in a little white alcove, where I cried myself to sleep after mother had left me at Tyler Hall; and when the last note of the blessed song climbed the masts, and the Baltimore rode alongside, the band struck up "Home Sweet Home." It was a signal for every man on the *Baltimore*. Their cheering drowned every other sound, while, from excess

The *Baltimore* homeward bound.

of joy, they swung their caps and threw them overboard. It was said that the bay was blue with them. I do not know. There was a mist came in just then, that made everything uncertain, except that the men of the *Baltimore* were going home, while we are anchored here for three long, long years.

A Rear-admiral came on the *Coptic*, and this morning an escort met him at the Grand Hotel, and brought him to the ship. Of course, every one was dressed in his best, the band was on the spar-deck,

The "Homeward Bounder".

the officers awaited him at the starboard gangway, the sailors stood attention, the marines presented arms. As the launch touched the gangway, the bo's'n piped the side, six Jackies fell in, forming an aisle at the top, and as the admiral stepped into it the whistle was answered by two rolls of the drum—the last rattle of which mingled with the flare of trumpets, that lustily played "Hail to the Chief." The Commander-in-Chief saluted the ship. The captain and flag-lieutenant stepped forward to greet him, escorting him aft to his quarters, while a rear-admiral's salute (thirteen guns) silenced the music of the band. While the salute* was firing, the pennant was

---

*A national salute...21 guns.   A vice-admiral's salute...15 guns.
  An admiral's salute...17 guns.   A rear-admiral's salute...13 guns.

The Rear-Admiral.

hauled down and the flag run up. A rear-admiral's flag is a blue field with two white stars upon it. An admiral's flag is the only flag that ever floats at night; but at sea, or in port, through all kinds of weather, so long as we carry an admiral, that flag will proclaim it. At night, and at sea, it will be not much larger than a cigar box; but it will bear two stars, and all the glory that goes with them.

Andy tells me that although the captain has lost his pennant, none of his glory has gone with it: he is still the grand mogul of the ship. The rear-admiral has command only of the fleet, and will probably give instructions to our captain in writing, as formally as he will to any other ship in the squadron.

Until today, I have honestly believed that the only being in America (off the stage) that could outshine a man-of-war's captain, with his cocked hat, gold lace and epaulets, was the captain of the marines; but the vision of a rear-admiral pales them all. In all his glory, I can liken him to nothing but a gold-plated Knight Templar.

A Rear-Admiral's flag.

For six months we have worn U.S.F.S. *Olympia* on our hat-bands, but this will be the first night we have slept on a real full-fledged, completely equipped *flag-ship*.

From ancient custom the captain is still called "the skipper"; the doctor is called "Microbes"; the carpenter, "Chips"; the chaplain, "Sky-pilot," etc., and because the admiral has nothing to do with our ship he is nicknamed "the Passenger."

A conscientious fulfilment of duty seems to be the life-aim of every officer of the navy. For illustration I will report our doctor. Our crew is so provokingly healthy that, for want of other practice, he has been vaccinating us all the way from San Francisco. It has become a regular routine; he keeps at a fellow until it *takes*. I can not say how many times I have been slashed; but, just as many as it is, that many times have I thoroughly washed it off with alcohol, and saved myself from the discomfort of a sore arm.

"The compliments of the season," seems to be tabooed on shipboard, for not a "Merry Christmas" did I hear; but there was a good dinner, and a free gangway. I celebrated by going to a wrestling match. Need not make note, as I can never forget those flabby human frogs, nor cease to wonder whence comes their strength.

One of Yokohama's boasted prides is its police force; still I know seamen who tell how they have taken their swords away from them, tossing them upon the roofs, just to see them go down on their knees in courteous salaams to their tormentors.

My own experience with them was on leaving the wrestling match on Christmas night. There was a gang of us, and as we walked along we heard a chorus of Japanese jargon, with a high note of undeniable, though not elegant English running through it. Following the note around the corner into a by-street, there was Billie, one of our sick-bay nurses. He is the smallest man on the ship, and at that moment was "All bound round with a woolen string"; while not less than seventeen policemen were tugging, in seventeen directions, at the ropes that bound him, while Billie, fighting like a demon, refused to go with them. At sight of our uniforms they dropped the ropes and took to their heels; and Billie, rejoicing in his liberty, climbed the waterspout of a two-story house, that he might crow from its eaves. Japan's architecture is not built for strength: the spout gave way. Such a commotion as it kicked up! The inmates rushed out, but we dragged our poor shipmate along, running like firemen, and never asking if his bones were broken. We reached the French hettaba, jumped into our boats, and reported on ship, with only one man marked D.D.—"drunk and dirty."

Ever since Columbus sailed the seas, there has existed a custom of ringing sixteen bells at the mid-watch on New Year's eve—eight are tolled for the departing, eight rung for the coming year. But the powers that rule have ordained that it shall be a misdemeanor to ring more than eight bells; nevertheless, there is not a man living who has been on ship at the birth of a New Year who has not counted sixteen strokes, but it is our only demonstration, and "Nobody says nothing to nobody."

Japan's New Year, however, follows close in our wake, and they certainly make up for any lack of enthusiasm on our part. Everybody gets up at "the hour of the tiger,"—four bells—2 A.M.—dresses in his richest raiment, and goes forth to greet the earliest dawn. Gifts are exchanged, everybody says to everybody else something that translates into, "Good luck for ten thousand years."

A foot of snow on the ground does not interfere with out-of-door fairs, and it is wonderful what a dazzling background the snow makes for the thousands of lanterns and torches that come out in the night.

My leave was for forty-eight hours; I was back on time, and saw the officer-of-the-deck check my name off the "liberty list" with O.T.C.S.—"On time, clean and sober."

We start for Nagasaki tomorrow.

CHAPTER VI

THE INLAND SEA

If Yokohama was disappointing in its modernness, Kobe has more than made up for it. It is as Jappy as a bamboo screen, an appropriate gateway to the Inland Sea, with its two hundred miles of enchanted waters set among rocky cliffs and wooded hills, while islands as varied as they are numerous rise from its glassy surface, and every spot is alive with a diminutive humanity. And when our great white ship, encircled with a scarlet band (the crest of the Asiatic squadron), came like a giant among Liliputians, from rice-field, grove, and temple, they came running to look upon us.

We were a day and a half passing through the sea, and for the first time I felt a regret when my night watch aloft was ended; and as I came down I was wishing James Lane Allen, the man who wrote the "Choir Invisible," might stand up there and write the story that the twinkling lights of the lanterns in the graveyards are telling.

Nagasaki proved indeed a fitting climax to the voyage. No matter who has written about it, one half of the beauty of Nagasaki Harbor has never been told. Every nation that floats a ship has a representative here, and the flaunting of the various flags, together with the firing of salutes, makes a veritable water carnival, and yet amid all this loveliness, Mess No. 3 had troubles of its own.

A mess on a man-of-war consists of twenty-four men, and is run in this manner:

Uncle Sam, through his quartermasters, issues monthly, nine dollars in rations to each enlisted man. Each mess has a cook and a caterer. The cook draws two rations, and is excused from all duties except drill. The caterer is elected each month, though if he prove satisfactory to the mess, and likes the job, he often holds it for a whole cruise. It is customary, when in port, instead of drawing full rations, to take from the ship only the staples, and one half in cash. Thus one hundred and eight dollars, plus one dollar from each man's pocket, makes a total of one hundred and thirty-two dollars, United States currency. This amount is given to the caterer, who spends it at his own discretion, rendering each month an account to his mess. With provisions at Oriental prices, we live much better than at college.

But there came a day when our mess fell to grief. It was just after pay-day. Our caterer had drawn our money, and he skipped ship. The consequence was we had to go down into our pockets to replenish our larder, which curtailed our shore-leave, for what can a Jackie do ashore without coin?

It is warmer here than in Yokohama, and Rear-Admiral McNair chose the place to do his first official stunt. It is called Admiral's Inspection, and lasts for two or three days. Talk about Sunday morning inspection! By comparison it has dwindled into a pleasant dream. The rear-admiral and his staff come forth as to battle. There is not the minutest detail of the ship nor its workings overlooked. We have drills of all sorts and kinds, by gun, small-arm, single-sticks and pistols; company battalion, arm and away, and everything else we can do with boat, oar, or sail. When they have added collision and fire-drill to the above, a flag-lieutenant comes along and goes through everything you own (excepting your diddy-box). To one man he says, "Bring your hammock," to another, "Your gun" etc. To one he said "Fetch your bag." Never have I been able to keep a closet or bureau in order. What order, then, could I be expected to keep in a bag? I felt the shadow of the brig creeping across me when I heard from my port, in *sotto voce*, "Take mine." God bless Andy! He is as neat and orderly as he is generous. It was taking desperate chances, but the flag-lieutenant had not been with us long, and when at my feet I opened up that model of bags with "Andy Burns" stenciled in big black letters across it, the lieutenant said, "Very neat, Andy, very neat," and passed on as our division officer followed him and said, soft and low, "More sense than I gave you credit for, but do not let it occur again."

"Sup-posey you."

"Sup-posey you," says all Japandom. At a tea-house where they serve excellent oysters I made free to call one of the girls Fuji. One day, getting there first and while waiting for the boys to come, the little lady came timidly to me and said, "Jack sen, sup-posey so, just you, just me talkey, sup-posey you call me Fuji all right. Please Jack a-sen sup-posey more sailor-man come you speakey me Fuji Sen." It amused me, and here on the ship sometimes just to while the time away I "sup-posey." For example, suppose a captain should go with an admiral to meet friends and have a good time on shore, and should leave his ship in charge of the lieutenant commanding. Then suppose the said "luff" should, in the temporary capacity of a captain, think the lieutenant commanding entitled to shore-leave and grant it to him. *Suppose* such a thing (though not probable, but altogether possible) should occur, what would be the result?

Lieutenant-Commander Sturdy left us without so much as a good-by. We thought him harsh sometimes, and always remembered our grievance at the Islands as being largely due to him, but now he is gone, every man is free to own that though exacting, no officer was ever more generous in the granting of shore-leave.

CHAPTER VII

MAN-O'-WAR POOL

The mariner who comes to Shanghai would find it difficult to define where the ocean leaves off and the river begins, and many are the ships that ride in and out with the tide. Therefore we moored stem and stern in Man-o'-war Pool, off Woo-song Fort, and from here made many visits to the ancient city. Our uniforms are a passport everywhere we go; still, in doing old Shanghai we generally take a Chinese guide, who wears a ribbonless sailor's cap. The sights I have seen I need not write for fear of forgetting, but I want to be forgiven for saying that leprosy had no horrors. To see living skeletons with iron bands about the neck or waist chained to a stone wall, piteously wailing and begging for food, is a spectacle that will haunt me as long as I live.

While I shall ever think of the Canton River as a beautiful kaleidoscope with its shifting colors of silken sails and pennants, such display of wealth is probably nowhere else to be seen. However, we have not spent all of our time sight seeing; we have been to Saddle Rock for drill and small-arm practice, shooting from the land at a moving target on the water, and from the ship's boats bobbing on the waves at a target on the cliffs.

Uncle Sam is more generous to the small-arm

shooting than in any other drill, giving cash prizes of five and ten dollars each. I have been quite a lucky winner, and am hoping that when we get to India some officer will see fit to take me into the wilds with him to shoot his tiger. I have always longed to shoot Japanese pheasants, and have finally been gratified. It was one day when in training for a boxing match that is waiting for us when we get back to Yokohama, that I was running along the levee, I came upon some English lords who wore proud hunting togs and were wasting good ammunition in the willows. The temptation was too great for me. I asked if I might take a shot. The result was I shook my trainer and stayed with the lords until their sacks were well filled and they had given me a string of them for our mess. I am almost sorry I did it, for, alluring as the anticipation of pheasant shooting has been, the reality is awfully like shooting hens in your grandmother's chicken-yard.

CHAPTER VIII

THE WRECK OF THE ON WOO

The waters of the Yang-tse-Kiang River have such a salutary effect upon barnacles that we lay well into its mouth, letting them drop away, saving Jackie from many a hard day at scraping.

It was four bells of the mid-watch on the thirteenth of April when Andy (*sans souci*) threw me out of my hammock as he called, "Jack, Jack, for God's sake be quick! Lots of men overboard!"

Thinking my shipmate had developed somnambulism, I caught him by the shoulders and shook him soundly as I screamed into his ear, "Wake up!" It was only a moment until the bo's'n's pipe rang shrill and he chantied (pronounced shan-teed) "A-l-l h-a-n-d-s up; A-l-l hands man the life-boat. Do you h-e-a-r that now!" And then all the search-lights were turned on and it was like day.

Early in the night a dense fog had drifted in from the ocean, and now the incoming tide was running a torrent whose angry lashings mingled with the shrieks and moans of dying men. What a sight it was to behold! The *On Woo*, a Chinese passenger steamer coming from up the coast on its way to Shanghai, had collided with a tramp freight schooner right at the mouth of the river and had sunk. It is estimated that between five and six hundred lives were lost.

At the time of the disaster we were undergoing repairs in the harbor; consequently our ship was almost surrounded by barges that served as temporary machine shops. To cut lose these barges in such a raging tide would have added wreck to ruin. The ship was so hemmed about that we were unable to lower more than two quarter-boats. The barges were manned with the hope to rescue those who floated past, but they were so high above the water that they saved but few, while standing eager but helpless, watching head after head bob above the surge only to be dashed out of existence against the barges' sides.

The two boats succeeded in saving thirty-eight lives, four of them being Europeans. For a time the water was as black with human beings as I have ever seen it with porpoises. When we had hauled as many into our boats as they would hold, others struggling for life would cling to our gunwales and to our oars and would have swamped us had we not resorted to the inhumanity of lifting the stretchers from the bottom of the boat and with them breaking the already benumbed fingers, thus forcing them to relax their last grip on life. In my boat one man died after we had taken him in. He was thrown overboard and another picked up in his place.

The admiral and the captain gave up their cabins to the women and children, and our surgeons ministered to them all.

Day dawned upon a sorry sight. The beach was strewn with the dead, and be it told to the shame of China that during the hours we were risking our lives to save her people hundreds of junks lay in the harbor,

Chinese junks.

Execution of pirates.

yet not a man lent a helping hand. In their belief it was a beatific sacrifice to the god of the waters, while to have rescued one would have been an indignity to that awful deity; moreover, it is decreed that if a man defy the water god when he asks for a human soul, he must forever after look out for its body. Thus, should A fall into the sea and B snatch him out, A may go to B and demand that he support him as long as he lives, because A would *not* have fallen into the sea had the water god not called him.

For days after the catastrophe, coolies would wade out into the water, and, thrusting their long-burden poles through the garments of the dead, pack and dump them in heaps upon the shore, and there the river pirates came, both men and women, and robbed the corpses.

After the third day we fired a six-inch gun several times across the water, and more corpses came to the surface. Oh, it was sickening!

The authorities finally set out to put an end to the pillage, which resulted in the capture of five pirates. Three of them were women, in the folds of whose turbans were found jewel-encircled fingers severed from the hands of the dead.

As soon as captured the men's cues were cut. The details that followed were consummated with a dexterity characteristic of all of Judge Lynch's decrees.

From the ship we could see them as plainly as one sees a theatrical performance from a proscenium-box. For a background to the pantomime (not a word was spoken) they chose a spot on the beach where the flaring-mouthed, green brass cannon of old fort Woo Song cast a frowning shadow. Here they brought the culprits. With hands tied behind them they knelt facing the sea, while the executioner with diabolical flourishes of his sword danced and pranced about them until, wearied by the exertion, he swung five fell swoops, and the white sand drank up the blood—ugh! I shall be glad when we get away from here.

ASIATIC STATION.

Squadron General Order,	}	U. S. Flagship OLYMPIA,
Number 2.		Woosung, China, May 1, 1896.

1. The Commander-in-Chief is gratified to he able to express his warm appreciation of the humane spirit and seamanlike ability of the officers and men of the Squadron present at Woosung, China, on the morning of the thirtieth of April, when, upon the occasion at the sinking of the steamer ON-WO, thirty-eight lives were rescued by the OLYMPIA, four by the YORKTOWN, and one by the BOSTON.

2. The promptness and skill of the officers and men of the OLYMPIA came directly under the notice of the Commander-in-Chief, and are testified to by the number of human lives that were saved. And while, owing to their greater distance from the scene of the disaster, the other vessels present were unable to take so large a part in the work of rescue, the Commander-in-Chief is equally pleased to extend to their officers and crews his congratulations upon the success of their efforts.

F. V. McNAIR,

Rear Admiral, U. S. Navy,
Commanding U. S. Naval Force on Asiatic Station.

CHAPTER IX

THE GREAT WALL OF CHINA—A BOAT-RACE

Latitude 36° N, Longitude 121° E, on the southern coast of the Bay of Korea, and just across from Port Arthur—this is Chi-fu, where we get our first glimpse of the Great Wall of China, an irregular brown line meandering over the hills and crumbling into the sea.

Most of our deep-sea drills were cut out of this trip, as we were kept busy looking after the ship; she was playing leap-frog with the waves all the way through the Yellow Sea, and Uncle Sam has figured it out that when it is too stormy for us to fight, the enemy will be riding on the same wave.

From eight bells until ten in the morning the first officer takes the deck, but since the departure of Lieutenant Sturdy, until we reached Chi-fu, we have not known for a certainty whom we should meet.

Swoop! Like a meadow-lark on a fence-rail he lit upon the deck, a dapper little man with his cap set at port aft, and his sword bristling with authority, we recognized on sight our new executive officer. Colors went off with a swing the *Olympia* has never know before, and while the echo of "The Star Spangled Banner" came back from the mainmast, Lieutenant Delano commanded, "Band-master, play 'Nancy Lee.'" Then to its rollicking strains he paced the deck. From that moment he has been known to the men as Nancy Lee. (To nickname an officer is one of the greatest compliments a crew of blue-jackets can pay him.)

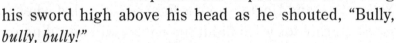

"Nancy Lee"

It takes an admiral to make a flag-ship. A captain can "Up sticks," but it is the first lieutenant, or "First Luff," as he is called for short, who leavens it all. From the moment Nancy Lee clanked his heels on the deck it has been like home; and when on Drill Island he gave the command, "Company left, form into line, battalion square," the readiness with which we executed it surpassed his expectation. He swung his sword high above his head as he shouted, "Bully, *bully, bully!*"

Drill Island! It makes my legs ache to write it, for I have tramped ten thousand miles (or less) over its rocky cliffs and sandy shores, dragging field-pieces, and playing soldier like boys on the Fourth of July. Since the day of my enlistment, on an average of once a week we have gone through a drill "Equip for heavy marching order." Each man runs to his hammock, unlashes, takes out his blanket, and lashes up again; from his bag he takes an extra suit of blue and one of white, with a lot of other things prescribed, and packs them in his knapsack, and whether he uses tobacco or not, there must be a plug brought along. He fills his cartridge-belt and buckles it on, ditto his canteen, ditto his leggings. In his haversack he puts a plate, cup, knife, fork and spoon. When ready with guns, battle-axes and brush hooks, he is carrying a load of about eighty pounds. Hurrying to the deck, there is generally a dress-parade, a flare of trumpets and all would be over until the next time.

It always seemed to me like a lot of unnecessary trouble, besides mussing one's clothes and soiling blankets. Therefore Smithy and I put our heads together and hit upon a labor-saving device. From some crumpled newspapers covered with the leg ends of a pair of Smithy's discarded blues we fashioned most creditable appearing dummy packs, which we kept stowed away in the hammock netting. It was a happy thought all right, and enabled us always to be among the first at the scuttle-butt with our canteens. But the first time Nancy Lee gave the drill, instead of keeping to the text we had learned so well he ordered the boats lowered. A man-o'-war's-man may never make excuse nor offer apology. There was nothing to do but to obey the command, that night on the Island, when we were ordered to "S-t-a-c-k arms, u-n-sling knapsacks, o-p-e-n." When the lieutenant looked at our packs he only smiled, realizing that we were inflicting our own punishment. As we remained on the island doing hard drill for nearly three days and sleeping on the ground at night, the remnant of white flannel that represented my blanket would have been insufficient for a bureau scarf.

In Chi-fu Harbor we found the *Charleston* and the *Yorktown*. With the former we exchanged men, she taking the short, we the long timers.

We have had a most exciting twelve-oar barge-race

between the *Charleston* and the *Olympia*. The ship's launches tow the racing boats three miles out into the stream. The fleet's ships are moored so that they pull to a finish between them and in full sight, and it *was* a sight worth seeing. It has left us with a full exchequer, and what is still better, *"The Cock of the Station."* The Cock of the Station is a flag of purple silk on which is embroidered, in the finest Oriental needleship, a big red rooster. Each time a race is won it goes to the victor, who adds a gold star to its field. Had we failed to win it from the *Charleston*, it would have been left on the station and given to the first ship that won, for whenever two or more of our ships lie in the same harbor, a boat-race is always in order.

Betting on sea sports is not an individual matter. Generally the master-at-arms starts out with a sack and a book. You put in as much as you like to risk, and he writes it down; all bets are even, and when the game or race is done, one ship or the other takes the sack. The winners get two to one for every dollar they put in, and the losers get—left, just as we are left again, for the *"Charlie"* is out on the waters, scudding home!

She left us, with the cock of the station, a lot of good fellows, but most of all I wish she had left us her *taps*.

The seas over, taps has always been "Go to bed, go to bed," excepting on the *Charlie*. There came a night when the bugler was absent. The deck officer called on a cornet player to sound taps.

"Don't know how, sir," answered the man.

"Great guns!" shouted the officer, "Can't you play some kind of a lullaby that will tell the men to go to hammocks?" Placing the instrument to his lips,

The boat-race between the crews of the *Olympia* and the *Charleston*.

"The Great Wall of China."

he played:

> I'm tired now and sleepy, too;
> Come put me in my little bed.

The captain came out to ask what it meant. Being told it was a substitute for taps, he said, "Make it so," and so it has remained on the *Charleston* from that day to this.

Chapter X

The word "South" always stands for hospitality, therefore we were surprised to find it to such a superlative degree in Russian Siberia, where icebergs were basking in May's sunshine. We are the first man-of-war to have visited Vladivostok since the *Marion*, and that is so long ago, no one has been able to tell me when. We were there by special invitation, to witness the celebrating of the Czar's coronation.

There is nothing inviting in the barren, unfertile landscape with its unattractive square buildings, nor pleasing in a people as coarsely dressed as their soldiers, whose uniforms are made from a material that resembles the lining of a saddle pad. They are all of a dull color, and all seem to be cut to fit one man. It is a barracks town, so we saw little beside the Army and Navy, and their hospitality. Not a man of them spoke English, nor could we *"insky";* still, we were made to understand that the town was thrown open to us. We walked into their houses and rode in their carriages. Not a penny could we spend either for eat, drink, or smoke.

Smoke! That recalls the Russian cigarette of San Francisco, an article of delight so foreign to the *real thing*, which tastes and smells as if it were made from the clippings of these fellows' whiskers. If I had a barrel full of them I could go back and knock Keeley out of business with his Cigarette Cure.

Unsightly as the picture is by day, the night of the celebration unveiled one never to be forgotten. The harbor, where all of Russia's shipping lay at anchor, was illuminated in a manner that probably surpassed all the water carnivals heretofore known. Every craft in the bay, battle-ship or fishing-smack, from its truck to its rail, was outlined in varicolored electric lights or hung with gaudy lanterns. Throughout the evening bands played from their decks and from the shore, and when it grew late a Czar's salute was fired from all the war-ships (our own guns joining), and then as darkness stole over the waters we spied on the barren cliffs, line after line, like glow-worms crawling, faint lights that grew and grew, until, to the delight of the beholder, Russia's great double-eagle blazed out in electric lights and dominated the scene. Although many miles away, it was a fitting tribute to the new Czar.

Admiral McNair, in expressing his delight to the Russian officers, suggested that there was yet one act necessary to make our happiness complete—i.e., that Russia liberate and turn over to us her prisoners, the seal-packing crew of the *Alert*.

Poor devils! They were a sorry six that came to us, having been imprisoned for nearly seven years they had not, until they boarded the *Olympia*, heard a voice they could understand; and, according to their own statement, their chief diet had been "tallow candles." The messes vied with one another in entertaining them from Vladivostok to Hakodate, where they fell in with old friends and companions.

Seamen tell you "There is no law of God or man north of 43°." Hakodate, on the Isle of Yezo, in the Straits of Sangar, is only one degree south, yet shows no sign of lawlessness. It is as green and crisp as a bed of lettuce, while the pretty little whaling and sailing craft, with their poetic names and artistic figureheads on each schooner, make one long to shoulder a rifle, jump on board of the *Snow Bird*, or the *Silver Crescent*, and sail away to the North Pole.

In the beginning of the cruise, "in my green, salad days," before we reached Honolulu, I realized that I was a thorn in the side of the boatswain's mate in the after guards, and I feel certain that this same "Boatsy Brown" spent all of his sober moments when off duty in studying up ways and means to render my life even more wretched than I had succeeded in doing myself.

Brown was a bully who had picked me (one of the youngest and greenest of the crew), as a safe target for his malice. Andy (my instructor) reasoned with me that he wasn't worth notice, and I kept that thought in my mind until one night, during our first

"The big-sailed *Snow Bird*."

call at Yokohama, with oaths I will not write, he finished haranguing me with, "—I'll jerk your arm out and beat you to death with it!"

It was the last straw! With one blow I knocked him

senseless against the rail. From that hour, whenever he spoke to me it was in this manner: "Now, Jack, my boy, it is your anchor watch tonight."

In the shuffle and deal of men at Chi-fu we lost Boatsy Brown. However, we drew a character from the *Yorktown*. It was Jack Weir, acknowledged the toughest and the best-hearted man in the navy. How long he has been in the service, no one knows: enlistment stripes are an age index, therefore, Weir refuses to wear his full complement, and one might guess at his age anywhere between twenty and eighty. He has long since filled the positions of coxswain and boatswain's mate, but prefers the berth of a seaman, as it carries less responsibility, and he has ceased to aspire higher than the fourth conduct class.

Before his coming I had looked upon Purdy, the captain of the hold, as the most ornate *cusser* afloat (barring a certain "Luff"), but the vocabulary of Weir! There never was on land or sea anything to compare with it. The first time I saw him was in port at Chi-fu. He and Scotty Ross were on their knees abaft the port gangway, throwing craps. Scotty, a man so mean that he detests himself, was winning. Weir's cap was pushed aft, displaying a face as scarred and fascinating as a topographical map; shaking the craps, he talked to them—"Blanketty blank, bones, don't refuse me this time!"

When a little chap I owned and loved a bull-terrier that every one else feared. Weir would fight a buzz saw, and I'm thinking if I ever needed him, he would fight for me.

It is June. We are on the Pacific, headed for Yokohama, and I feel so queer. Can it be that I am ill?

CHAPTER XI

MAN-O'-WAR COCKTAILS

It is two months since I wrote the last chapter. The ship's surgeon settled my wonderment by quarantining me with five others up in the mainmast, where we spent a day and a night before coming into port, and before reveille on the following morning we were lowered into a cutter and towed ashore.

These details are less vivid to me than a troubled dream; they were followed by weeks of oblivion, for I was paying the penalty of my arm washings in the old vaccination days. It was smallpox all right, and probably contracted in Vladivostok. However, the contagion did not spread beyond the original six, and in no case proved fatal nor left us pock-marked.

Uncle Sam is a mother to his sailors when they are sick. The U.S. Naval Hospital is situated on Yokohama's bluff in the midst of its most aristocratic European colony. Beautiful courts with fountains and flowers make an environment that the convalescent is loth to leave. The physicians and nurses are both efficient and attentive, while every delicacy one might demand in a private sanatorium is gratuitously meted out. Should the admiral himself get ill he will be taken to the Naval Hospital, but it will be impossible for him to receive better care than that bestowed upon a blue-jacket.

As I was leaving the hospital I met one of our crew coming in. He said to me, "Shipmate, it's up sticks with me. I am losing my mind."

"Man-o'-war cocktail!" I replied, for I remembered it was he who introduced it to me when we came in last fall. He told me it was the life assurance of a tenderfoot in a cold climate.

A man-o'-war cocktail is made by putting one can of condensed milk in a gallon of hot water; pouring one quart of alcohol over six well-beaten eggs, adding two cups of sugar and some nutmeg (if you can get it). The result is a concoction that tastes not unlike a Christmas egg-nog, but the aftermath is very different. The night I drank of it I awoke with torture racking every bone of my body. My legs were so stiff I feared paralysis. The symptoms were so new to me that I attributed the cause to the potion I had drunk, and from that hour, cut it out. The pains have never returned, but I am a very small fraction of a ship's crew, and my withdrawal has in no degree diminished either supply or demand for man-o'-war cocktails.

The boys told me that after Joe had been taken to the hospital one of the black-gang found a five-gallon alcohol can half empty hidden away in the coal-bunkers. He had been drinking it straight. Poor fellow! Word came next day that he had died in the night. I heard that his brain was shrunken and withered like an apple with dry rot. (An eloquent lecture on alcoholism.)

The alcohol question has an amusing as well as a tragic side. The old navy doled out grog every day as a preventative of drunkenness. The custom was abolished,

"Quarantined in   the mainmast."

"The great double-eagle of Russia."

At Vladivostok—"We rode in their carriages."

and today every man who comes over the port gangway is searched like a thief. The old bravado, "As lief have the game as the name," has in many cases resulted in petty larceny. The ship carries a beautiful mahogany chest whose key is kept by the master-at-arms. From its recesses he gives out the alcohol used in shellacking the decks. It is in this connection I recall an amusing incident which implicates Jack Caldwell, who, according to his own oft-repeated declaration is "The best little man on the ship; on the jump from morning till night." (His shipmates will add, "Always in a fight, and always getting licked.") Well, after the shellacking of the deck is done there is always some of the mixture left in the pan. One day Caldwell conceived the happy thought to set it aside to settle, and, carefully pouring off the top, drank with a gusto. Result? How I wish I had Caldwell's picture to show you! The morning following his drinking of the stuff he came to quarters with every hair in his big mustache bristling. His mouth was drawn starboard and glued there, and his little eyes blinked sadly. It may not write funny, but he was a sight that nearly broke up quarters.

About two hundred and fifty miles north of Yokohama there is a break in the coast range. One cannot discern it from the ocean, as the walls from the north creep in behind the southern cliffs. From the ship it appears impregnable, but with a whale-boat flying an ensign, and our officers in full uniform, we one day pulled toward a bamboo pole standing white against the cliff. From this we espied another bamboo marking-pole, and yet another. Zigzagging from one to the other, we pulled through the channel into the port of Kuruchinama.

(Your-a-shing-hammer, we call it for short.) No cunning of man could ever have fashioned this place. It is a "closed port," and we were not permitted to step out of the boat, although our officers were ashore for a couple of hours. It was an official visit whose purport I never knew, but the enchantment of the surroundings are mine. We were in a lovely valley cradled among the green hills, from whose fastnesses a river ran, wide and deep, parting and meeting again about a wooded island, where temple and lantern rendered it as charming as the parks of Tokyo. On the other margin of the river villages and fortifications cluster about each other. We counted no less than six modern Japanese torpedo-boats sleeping on the water. If in hiding they are surely safe "in their cozy corner lying."

This visit to Kuruchinama was merely an incident; we were out for practise, and practise we did. If we are not now fitted for any kind of a sea performance we certainly are for dress rehearsal. We have abandoned ship so often, that if the real thing ever comes I do not believe we shall recognize it until water and provisions give out.

The man who volunteers to fall overboard that we may test the life-buoys, lower the boats, and rescue him while the ship is under way in mid-ocean, is paid two dollars each time. It is Bill Bartley who generally does this stunt, and it would be difficult to find another so well fitted to the role. With years of service in the fourth conduct class, Bill has learned the art of jumping ship and swimming for life and shore-liberty.

Since leaving Drill Island I had not seen my leggings until this morning, when I bid them in for ten cents. It was lucky-bag day. If you want to know what the lucky-bag is, just drop for a minute anything you own, and see how the master-at-arms will pounce upon it. If you really cannot get on without it you may go to him and redeem it by doing ten hours extra duty; other wise it remains "in hock" until the bag is so full it will hold no more; then, wherever or whenever this happens, he brings it

"Bill Bartley, the *Olympia's* regular 'man overboard.'"

up, dumping the contents on the deck, and a spirited auction ensues. I have seen a new flannel shirt that cost three dollars bid in for twenty-five cents. Also in a spirit of fun I have known an odd shoe to be bid up as high as five dollars; the owner determined to have it, his shipmates equally bent on making him pay for it. But there is always a lucky-bag day ahead, and accounts keep pretty even.

The third of November will be the Mikado's birthday and we are going back to Yokohama to salute him.

CHAPTER XII

It is customary for a man-of-war to fire a national salute (twenty-one guns) whenever she enters a foreign port. This time in entering Yedo Bay we were requested to waive the salute, probably because we come so often it is like one of the family coming home to dinner.

The Emperor's birthday was so very similar to three hundred and sixty-four other festivals annually celebrated in Tokyo that it is not worth chronicling. I saw their Royal Highnesses, the Emperor and the Empress but so have millions of others, and the pageant impressed me less than a little affair of my own that subsequently occurred.

I was on signal watch on the after-bridge; an ordinance officer four feet away stood looking shoreward through his binoculars as the admiral's barge rowed straight for the ship. At the proper moment he commanded: "Bugler, call the guard." Then all the red tape required to get an admiral aboard was unwound. This accomplished, Lieutenant Dorn came at me fairly foaming at the mouth, "What are you doing on the bridge?" he roared.

"I am on signal watch, sir."

"Then why did you not report the admiral's launch coming?"

"Because you saw it, sir."

"Because *I saw it!* What right have *you* to say I saw it?"

"I saw you looking at it through your glasses, sir."

"You don't *know* that I was looking at the admiral's barge; you have no right even to *think* what I am looking at. Your duty was to have reported to me what you saw coming toward the ship. Failing to do so, you shall answer to the stick* on Saturday morning. I put you down for carelessness, disobedience, neglect of duty, and insolence."

I swallowed my rage, as I have done many a time and oft since I have worn this uniform, and, in fancy,

"In the brig."

saw myself go down into the brig for thirty days. The brig means handcuffs or ankle irons, a diet of two hardtacks, and a tumbler of water three times a day, with full rations every fifth day. I have seen men come out of the brig looking like the end of a forty-days' fast in a monastery. I have seen men in for three days wearing double irons. They looked like pirates. Their crime was *smoking out of hours.*

The brig is losing popularity since Nancy Lee came, his motto being: "Give sailors plenty of work and plenty of feed."

---

*Answer to the stick: or called to the mast where the officer-of-the-deck receives the men who wish to speak with him.

To return to my own case. On Friday night Lieutenant Dorn sent for me and gave me a kindly talk, winding up with the promise that he would either make a sailor out of me or kill me. I was on the shore list for the next morning, but for reasons of my own tarried on the ship. This same officer, noticing me, asked why I was there.

"Broke, sir," I answered.

He told me to go to his room and where to find ten dollars, which I was to take, get ashore as quickly as possible, and not to forget to return it on the next pay-day.

You may be sure I did return it, and now that I have a berth on the admiral's launch I will always be out when it is. And I have learned this: a man may be your neighbor even though he employ a different tailor.

Periodically a tattoo fever breaks out on ship. It is raging now, and has left me with a pretty little geisha girl on my port forearm. Speaking of tattooing recalls the finest specimen I have ever seen. It was during the warm season when we were wont to go to Homoca, swimming. I saw a Japanese gentleman there whose whole body, excepting his head and hands, was completely incased, as it were, in the skin of a dragon. Sailors are restricted to two colors, red and blue, they being least likely to produce blood-poisoning; but this man was done in so many colors that when his body was wet and shining I could compare him to nothing else than a great satsuma jar with a human head. His loin-cloth was always a bit of rare oriental silk that contrasted harmoniously with the

A geisha girl

dragon hues. It made me wish that Adam and Eve had foregone the apple and that we had all been born with an ornamental epidermis.

Think what a lot of trouble and expense it would have saved!

Immodest? Not a bit of it. He looked fit to go to court.

The snow that came with the glamor of newness last year was earlier this season and seemed cold, dull, and prosaic. Filled with emotions kindled of these conditions, alone one Saturday night I strolled through Bloodtown. From across the street the hum of English voices floated out upon the night air. Forgetting that our glorious nation ever had a mother, I crossed over and threw open the door whence issued the sounds. Biff! Bang! I was out in the mud and the snow, my nose bleeding, my lips cut and my best uniform so soiled and bespattered that I was unfit for presentation at the Salvation Barracks.

I was the victim of a whole squad of English blue-jackets. How I prayed for a gang of our own, but they came not! Recognizing the futility of an attempt to redress my wrongs single-handed, I strolled back to the hettaba, where from excess of wrath and mortification I sat down and cried, cried as only a defeated man can cry. My tears spent, I sat waiting for the first boat returning to the ship, when I heard another song. It was a good old gospel hymn, hummed soft and low, its aspirated h's proclaiming the singer an Englishman, and the lights on the hettaba proving him to be a sailor. What did I do? I am ashamed to write it, for I well-nigh beat the life out of him.

Next morning, after church, our sky-pilot announced

that he had received word from the chaplain of an English warship that one of their men, while returning from a meeting of the Y.M.C.A., had been cruelly beaten by a U. S. man-o'-war's man. Our chaplain made it a point that he did not think it was done by one of the *Olympia's* boys, mentioning it only because it had been brought to his notice. However, had he known it was I, there was nothing for him to do. When a sailor is on shore he is his own boss—*His own boss!* I am just awaking to that fact. It was the desire to be my own boss more than anything else in the world that sent me to sea. Oh, the irony of it!

Chapter XIII

A Banquet

November was drawing to a close when we left Yokohama, again passing through the enchanted Inland Sea on our course to Nagasaki. Our anchor chains had not ceased rattling when we espied the Russian battleship, *Rurik*, in port. It was the chance of our lives; it was an opportunity to repay in a measure some of the hospitality showered upon us when in Vladivostok.

Purdy proposed that we play "Uncle Tom's Cabin," or "Twelfth Night," for them, but after long and mature deliberation it was decided that, owing to the differences of dialect in the two navies, the only appropriate entertainment must be one to appeal equally to guest and host. Plain as the nose on your face. Nothing but a banquet.

The decision formed, our captain granted twenty-four hours' shore liberty to one hundred picked men from the *Olympia*. A corresponding number of invitations were sent to and accepted by the blue-jackets of the *Rurik*.

Then came the appointing of our committees; committee on hall decoration, music, and refreshments. Not a detail was slighted, and when the auspicious evening arrived we met at the dock in single files, there forming into double lines, two by two, a Russian and an

American. Thus we marched to the scene of festivities. The bands from both ships preceded us, and occupied the stage, above whose central arch the flags of America and Russia were draped gracefully amid the feathery branches of Japanese ferns.

Alternately the national airs of the two great nations mingled with the mirth and laughter of the feast. We had two hired interpreters, and the toasts exchanged were all couched in terms of extravagant praise. (In secret pride each Yankee looked upon the spread of dainty viands, contrasting them with the coarse food we had partaken of in the homes of our guests.)

It was Chalmers who suggested the favors, and it was he who set the example for their proper disposal. At each place, alternating, was a tiny American or a Russian flag. As soon as seated, Chalmers pinned a Russian flag above his heart. The spark caught; in a twinkling every flag on the table rested upon an alien bosom, and all went

Tar and banjo.

merry as a marriage feast, when suddenly, all unannounced, a great whiskered "Insky" arose with a wine-glass in his hand. He was excitedly declaiming, and before any one had caught his purport he had shattered the goblet and spilt the wine, torn the American ensign from his breast, and would have trampled upon it had not his American partner anticipated the act and felled him to the ground.

It was the signal. Every man tore off his favor, and

if there was in the assembly an American brain clouded with the red of the wine it cleared when his flag was insulted. A bloody man-to-man war ensued. We fought until we overflowed the hall and spilled into the streets. The band-men fled in terror. The authorities grasped the situation and closed all of the public houses.

The first fray over, memory recalled the unfinished dinner, and all night long, singly and by the dozens, guests and hosts returned to the banquet-hall, and when the sun came dripping out of the east he saw a thoroughfare of Nagasaki besprinkled with sleeping sailors and with flags like confetti after Mardi Gras.

Nothing to say, my darling;
Nothing at all to say.

Like last year, Christmas consisted of roast turkey and a free gangway.

A week later I was alone on shore fighting the ghosts that always cluster about my life's milestones, when I grew to watching the lights come on in the swinging signs, flashing invitation to the sailorman.

There were the Main Top, Fore Top, Naval Club, Forecastle, Flag of All Nations, Man at the Wheel, and The Land We Live In.

From an open space above the swinging screen of the last came the most doleful chorus, the most melancholy rendering of the "Star Spangled Banner" I ever expect to hear.

Recalling my little experience in Yokohama, I warily chinned myself until I could look over the green baize. There was Bill Phelan (three sheets in the wind) with a club in his hand and a squad of English blue-jackets backed against the bar, their spokesman protesting, "But we don't know your bloody 'ymn, don't you knaw."

"Never mind, you bloody devils, you'll know it all right when I get through with you. Now all together. 'Oh, say, can you see—'"

This was too good. I ran back to the Naval Club and returned with an audience that crowded for standing room in the saloon. After they had mastered "The Star Spangled Banner" the audience turned in and helped Bill out with his entertainment. We taught them to sing "Hail, Columbia," "Yankee Doodle," and "America." The last being set to the same music as "God Save the King," was such a howling success that we concluded it was a fitting finale for the evening's entertainment. Besides, the singers were so hoarse that their voices grated, and midnight was striking. We allowed them to treat the crowd, drinking with us to the good ship *Olympia* and to the New Year 1897.

CHAPTER XIV

HONG KONG—A THIEF

To my benighted intellect Hong Kong had always been a Chinese metropolis. Conceive, then, the shifting my gray matter had to undergo when I found an island, seven by two miles in extent, lifting a rocky promontory to a height of two thousand feet above the estuary of the Canton River.

Victoria, its chief port, has a colossal statue of the good English queen Victoria standing in the square, and is as British as a monocle. In short, it is a European city with Oriental embellishments, chief among them being its police force, composed mainly of Sikhs and Chinese. And once let a Chinese cop lay on hands, it is all up with you. There is Henderson, a great big State of Maine man, who employed his shore-leave in breaking up a drinking house. In consequence he is at present serving a ninety days' sentence in packing shot in a Hong Kong prison. Uncle Sam never interferes with the fate of his subjects when they disregard the laws and rights of foreigners. (A slip of my pencil: *we are the foreigners.*)

Going out to Happy Valley is like visiting the Cliff House, Sutro's, Burlingame, Tanforan and the Presidio golf links all in one. It is the playground of Hong Kong, and as after play comes rest, it is befitting that the

Kuruchinama.

Hong-Kong.

cemeteries are close by. In one of them lie the mortal remains of Miller. The sexton, in pointing out the graves of celebrities, always says, "Here lies Boatswain Miller, the Ananias of America's Navy." The epithet in no degree reflects disparagingly upon the memory of the departed, but serves rather as an incentive for such men as Seaman McCue, Scotty Ross, Jack Weir and others whose tales of the sea are as varied as they are interesting.

Of Miller, be it known that had he blown a boatswain's pipe as many years as he spun yarns about, he must have spent a century on the deep, while the stories ascribed to him would fill a volume. Two of them I am going to write lest I forget them.

Once upon a time, long years ago, Miller, who was boatswain of the *Franklin* carrying the flag of Admiral Farragut, fell overboard from a ship that drew eighteen feet of water. The life-preservers were cast to him, and in a twinkling he came dripping up the gangway with a grating under each arm. The skipper was the first man he met, and in excited accents he said, "Captain, if I haven't been treading bottom for the last half hour you may call me a——liar."

This is what *they* say. But the story he told most often was of a time when he was in Cape Town. Entering a saloon, he recognized at the bar a number of British officers. Being of a retiring nature, he was quietly backing out, when one of them recognized him and called out, "Come in, come in." He begged them to excuse him, reminding them that they were her Majesty's commissioned officers, while he was merely Boatswain Miller of the United States Navy. With minutial detail he was wont to repeat what each one said, what *he* said, and how finally he yielded to their gracious entreaty on condition that *they drink with him*. The terms were accepted, and as he was paying for the beer one of the party took him by the hand and said:

"Boatswain Miller, I have heard of you, and am proud to have made your acquaintance. I am not only an officer in the Queen's Navy, but I am the Duke of Edinburgh, and I want you to remember that the next time we meet you are to drink a bottle of wine with me."

Months dragged into years. There was not a man on the seas who had not heard of the honor awaiting Boatswain Miller. He told his story so often that it threatened to run into rhyme, and then it came about that Miller again sailed away to Cherbourg, and it really happened that the Duke of Edinburgh was to visit his ship. When the day and the hour of his coming arrived, the ship was dressed in a rainbow, the marine guard stood attention, and Boatswain Miller piped the side as the duke came up the gangway. But no look of recognition crossed his face. Admiral Farragut met him, and together they walked aft to his cabin. Immediately they were inside, the duke begged the admiral to tell him if anything was wrong with his uniform. Assured that every detail was perfect, he said that he was positive every man he had passed, not excepting the marines, showed marked signs of suppressed laughter.

It was an opportunity for Admiral Farragut to relate the story Miller had been repeating for twenty years. Listening to the end, the duke begged the admiral to furnish him with a bottle of champagne and permit him to finish the joke.

When a messenger told Boatswain Miller he was

wanted in the captain's cabin, all felt that his hour of reckoning had arrived. They felt sure he had gone into the presence of the duke that he might be made to "eat his words."

He was not gone long, and, returning, was seen to wipe his mouth on the back of his hand as he swaggered up to the officer-of-the-deck and said, "Me and the duke has just drank that champagne. I suppose you fellers thought I was a liar."

There come moments of seriousness and of reflection into the lives of all men, and if ever in one of these Miller had doubted the truth of his own story that moment had flown, never to return. Had not the duke in drinking with him in the sacred presence of the admiral confirmed his story?

"Honor among thieves" has its parallel in "honesty among sailors." I would unhesitatingly put any amount of money in my diddy-box in the presence of the whole crew, but the landsman is not always so safe, as was proved in the case of a bumboatman who had a silk neckerchief stolen from his pack when peddling on our ship more than a year ago in Yedo Bay. The thief was detected and put into the brig to await trial.

I had quite forgotten the occurrence until we were piped "A-l-l h-a-n-d-s to muster, to hear the sentence of a thief. Do you hear that now?" Of the trial I am ignorant. What we heard this morning ran something like this:

"For on the morning of the thirteenth of November, 1895, with malice aforethought, etc."

The sentence passed, his bag and baggage including full pay from the hour of his detection, were brought to him; a guard escorted him to the port gangway;

here the officer-of-the-deck took his cap, and, stripping it of its ribbon, returned it to him. It is an indignity a sailor-thief can never escape. With head bowed in shame he entered a boat and was rowed away to the shore, where he will probably join the ranks of that little army whose

Disgraced.

recruits represent almost every civilized nation under the sun. I mean the beach-combers.*

*Beach-comber: A seafaring man, generally of vagrant and drunken habits, who idles around the wharves of seaports.

CHAPTER XV

We found Bangkok and Singapore right where Rand and McNally have located them on the map. With a sieve Bangkok might be separated into two pictures; one so ugly I am fain to pass it by. The other a brilliant carnival of nations whose booths were floating shops and markets, a little Venetian waterway under the shadows of quaint old pagodas. Our stay was short, and as we journeyed on toward Singapore and it kept getting hotter and hotter, I wished we had tarried longer at Bangkok, if only that I might have asked if it were the birthplace of the Siamese twins.

Singapore is only one degree north of the equator, and I was not disappointed that my anticipated tiger hunt was not to be realized. Nobody went, and as I always abominated crawling things, I spent a good part of my shore-leave dodging snake-charmers.

The people are interesting, to be sure, and it was novel to see a face blacker than seven black cats shut up in the coal-bunkers, crowned with a shock of Rufus red hair, while a European hat, coat, and waistcoat looked unique when the legs of the wearer were swathed in an uncut trousers pattern.

As in the Bowery, one sees strange things in Singapore. Personally I enjoyed most of all watching elephants building a railroad. The intelligence they displayed was little short of marvelous.

Of course every sailor had to take a ride on an elephant's back, but I was very glad when it was over. I felt like a fly on a shaky mold of jelly.

I could write a chapter on jugglers if I understood their faking. Ten days constituted our visit to Singapore, and there was rejoicing when we hove up anchor to return to Hong Kong and Mirs Bay.

Mirs Bay is about forty miles north from Hong Kong, on the coast of China, and in the great plan of the universe must have been designed especially for drills. It is large enough to float the navy of a nation; there is no landing; nothing to obstruct our range; an ideal place to try our torpedoes.

Our eight-inch guns are supposed to carry their projectiles eight miles, while the torpedo's distance is measured by feet. The moment a torpedo strikes the water it sinks to a level about six feet beneath the surface, the concussion awakening the infernal machine inside of her. Like a flash of lightning away she goes.

A torpedo.

Everybody knows what happens to the object that gets hit by a torpedo, but it was new to me to learn that in practice the battlehead is shut up on board in the magazine, and a dummy-head substituted. The torpedo, whose machinery is driven by compressed air under pressure of 400 pounds to the square inch, travels under water for a distance of eight hundred yards or more, then with a p-f-f that causes a splurt of the water, it comes to the surface. A launch goes after and tows her back. She has the air-chamber recharged and is fired again and again. Each one of these little toys costs our good Uncle twenty-five hundred dollars. The second one we fired balked, sunk clean out of sight, and never came up.

It was the opportunity for a diving drill. We are equipped with a full diving apparatus of six armors, the wearing of which is non-compulsory. When the torpedo sank I was among the volunteers to go searching.

Someone sang,

"Down in a diving-bell
At the bottom of the sea,"

but there were none of the sights and wonders Jules Verne depicted; just mud and slime and a terrible bugaboo feeling, especially when one gets underneath the ship. Of all the horrors the human mind can conjure, none can compare with the feeling that seizes one when he sees a man in diving armor coming toward him down under the ship. It is like an onslaught from the Royal Goblin of the deep. Seeing one coming at me, I signaled to be returned on deck, where I gracefully relinquished my suit to another eager volunteer, omitting to own that I had been frightened half out of my senses by a creature exactly like myself. One time in life when it was not well to "see oursel's as ithers see us."

We searched for two days, but, failing to recover the torpedo, quit Mirs Bay and went on an official trip to

Signal practice on the *Olympia*.

Chemulpo, in Korea. The only thing that impressed me there was that the Koreans wore padded or quilted coats, which, once put on, are never taken off, but suffered to fall to pieces, shedding bits of cotton over the landscape like down from a pussy-willow in springtime. When this moulting leaves them chilly they add a new garment on top of the others.

We remained only a week and were glad to be back in Nagasaki in time for the Cherry Blossom Festival. Oh, these children of Japan, how they adore nature and her bloom! It set me thinking of the many things they have learned from us in the last fifty years, and I am asking *why* we have not from them learned flower worship?

Year after year Americans flock here by the steamer-load to attend this fête, which is as a stanza sung to the accompaniment of the sami-sen in comparison with a grand opera poured from the golden throats of ten thousand orioles in the springtime of California.

California's spring! Is there on the face of God's creation anything to compare with it? The eschscholtzias, brilliant as the sun that bathes them, spread their gorgeous carpet over miles upon miles of valley and hillside, while the orchards growing above them wave flowery branches that shed with their dropping petals a perfume like the breath of angels. Must one go so far away from home to realize its beauty?

From Nagasaki we again went cruising. That is what we are out here for. Somewhere out on the deep—I did not note the latitude nor longitude, but we were far out from sight of land—the lookout shouted: "Sail O!" Through the binoculars it proved to be a Chinese fishing-schooner flying a house-flag and an international signal of distress.

One of our ship's Chinese servants was called to hail them through the megaphone. No answer returning, a boat was lowered, and, with the Chinaman as interpreter, rowed to her. She had been blown out to sea in a squall, lost her bearings, and for days had been completely becalmed. Her provisions and water had given out and the crew reduced to a pitiable condition. Their tongues were so swollen that they could not articulate a sound. Our surgeon ministered to their distress; we gave them water and rice and restored their bearings.

Out on the trackless it is not an uncommon sight to see a hulk, mast and spar gone, half filled with water, cradling on the waves. Now I know whence they come.

Chapter XVI

SONG

The Kearsarge *and the* Alabama

It was early Sunday morning
in the year of sixty-four.
The *Alabama* she cruised out
along the Frenchman's shore.
Long time she cruised about,
long time she held her sway,
But now beneath the Frenchman's shore
she lies in Cherbourg Bay.

CHORUS

Hoist up the flag, boys.
Long may she wave!
God bless America,
The home of the brave!

This is one of about forty verses of an historic ballad. Old Purdy hums them over as he attends to his light duties as captain of the hold, or occasionally by request,

119

sings them out lustily at the dog-watch. When Seaman McCue chances to be in a spiritous turn of mind he joins in the chorus.

Purdy and McCue! Living relics of the greatest naval battle of our Civil War. It is thirty-three years since they fought, one on the *Kearsarge*, the other on the *Alabama*. They were young men then, each defending a principle.

Seamen Purdy and McCue
fighting their battle over again.

McCue was of the number picked up out of the water by the English yacht, *Deerhound*, when the *Alabama* went down with her flag of truce. The destruction of his beloved ship left a wound on the heart of the seaman that never healed. The war ended. Returning to his native land, he found the Confederacy dead and buried while a vital longing for the sea was consuming him. Reasoning that, though wronged, he had always been an American, he enlisted in the United States navy, where he has remained in uninterrupted service ever since.

Seaman McCue (as he insists upon being called) is a little man with bright blue eyes peeping like spring violets through snowdrifts, for his hair and beard have retained the abundance of youth, though silvered to whiteness by the spray of the fleeting years. How many they have numbered none dare to ask, as Seaman McCue's distaste for age is made manifest whenever he speaks of his old shipmates now serving on the *Independence.* They are invariably referred to as "the Guardo Stiffs." Poor old seaman! It will break his heart, but I sadly fear this will be his last cruise. He is efficient in his duty,—sweeping the starboard side of the gun-deck, where his life is rendered as miserable as a pack of young sea devils can make it. As fast as he sweeps someone tears and scatters papers after him just to hear him swear, and yet when the day came that we noticed Mac totter on the boom, and he took to coming from the cutter by the gangway, it was whispered he would be exchanged to one of the ships going home—it was then his tormentors came to his rescue.

They begged the officer to excuse him from pulling an oar, as someone off duty would do it for him. The officer hesitated a moment, when Young, editor of the *Bounding Billow,* the ship's paper, and one of the keenest thorns that had pricked him, jumped into the old man's place, and, lifting his oar, said, "I will pull for Seaman McCue for one hundred years."

Mac has never uttered one word of thanks. Indeed, he showed much the same disposition he did on the morning of Admiral McNair's first inspection. Coming upon him in the ranks, the admiral said: "Well, Seaman McCue, I think it about time we old fellows should be excused from duty." But I think the act of Young entered into his heart, for, although there was little perceptible change in his general bearing, I think he went oftener to church, and I am sure he responded more willingly to the boys entreaty for a sea yarn.

Of Purdy? He must have been a giant when he

manned the guns of the *Kearsarge*, but today he is bent at the waist, and the surfs of time have whitened him even as they have his shipmate.

One's first sight of Purdy is startling, for in the middle of a high forehead there gleams a bright blue star, visible and outward sign of the star gang.

After the victory over the *Alabama*, twenty of the *Kearsarge* crew in solemn covenant swore they would never desert the navy while Uncle Sam had a plank afloat, and to render the vow binding they each consented to be tattooed in a manner that would unfit them for any other station in life. Purdy is the only member of the gang I have seen. I understand there are five or six of them still on the sea.

These men are not only living relics of a great battle; they are animated encyclopedia of the navy, looking with small favor on modern warfare, jumping at an opportunity to refer to the good old times when they had "iron men and wooden ships," leaving the inference that we are wooden men on iron ships. These are two of our veterans quietly filling the niches that Time has carved for them; but it is only necessary for some jolly young tar to say: "Today is the nineteenth of June," directly the dead embers of dissension kindle into a flame amidst whose crackling may be heard the hissing sound of "rebel," "liar," "white flag," and "traitor," intermingled with seamen's curses—an unfailing prelude to a rough-and-tumble, hand-to-hand fight that might continue to the bitter end were it not that the tormentors who start the fray always step in and separate them. The next day they are as good friends as ever.

It is entirely out of deference to these veterans that I

THE BOUNDING BILLOW.

PUBLISHED IN THE INTERESTS OF AMERICAN MEN-O'-WARSMEN

| Published at intervals on U. S. F. S. Olympia. | MANILA, PHILIPPINE ISLANDS, JUNE, 1898. | VOL. I. NO. 5. |

THE BATTLE OF MANILA BAY.

"We Came! We Saw! We Conquered!"

1776

LIBERTY

*"'Twas for Cuba and our honor, to avenge our heroes slain,
That victory wreathed our banner when we fought the ships of Spain."*

The *Olympia's* paper.

have had the *Kearsarge* and the *Alabama* tattooed on my right arm. And it is these good ships that will bear me, when I am old, away from the humdrum of life's cares back to the blue, blue ocean where I will set me down to rest upon the fluke of a kedge anchor and hearken again to the simple stories told in good faith by Neptune's own sons. I will listen to Seaman McCue's deep sea voice as he tells again that he goes to church, not because he believes the Lord is always there, but because He *might* drop in during divine service, and when the roll was called he would hate to salute and answer "Absent, sir."

But his faith in the divine presence on the old frigate *California* is like adamant. Mac was on her for three years, and during that time neither tide nor current had the least influence upon her; anchor where they might, contrary to all natural laws she always turned her stern to the stream. What caused it? Nothing but the presence on board of the Savior of Men, Who was so angry when the proud ship was ignominiously sold into civil service that He then and there forsook her, and from that hour she turned about and swung with the stream just like other ships. Should one manifest a doubt he will say, "I suppose you would dispute the coming of Paddy White's ghost for his Christmas rum on the *Independence*, even if you saw him with your own eyes flying like a white crane out of the cemetery back of the old powder magazine."

And when I have smiled again at these homely tales from the lips of McCue I will recall that it was Purdy who first opened my eyes to a full understanding of the distress of the Ancient Mariner.

It is his firm belief (and he is not alone in it) that in every bird of the sea there dwells the immortal soul of a sailor.

Whenever I see the old man silently watching the sea-fowls as they skim over the waters I know that he is communing with his old shipmates. These hallucinations are so perfectly harmless, so rapturously enchanting, that I gave rein to my own fancy, and in its flight I recognized in the black-ringed gull upon the foretruck the reincarnation of the bo's'n of the *Kearsarge*, and in the whispering winds in the rigging heard him shout: "Cast loose and provide," just as he piped on the morning of June 19, 1864.

On the morning of June twentieth, as our flag broke at the masthead, there was a whirr like a flock of birds taking flight, as the one hundred and one flags requisite to the dressing of a ship flew to their wonted places with England's ensign at our fore. It was the Queen's Jubilee, and such a cannonading Yedo Bay had never known before.

On the Fourth of July, twenty-second of February, and when we enter a foreign port, twenty-one guns are fired, and we have nothing better to offer were President McKinley to come aboard tomorrow; but on the morning in question, with the *Olympia* a tiny factor in a great pageant, Nancy Lee came on deck with sixty beans in his hand. Tossing them one by one away, he marked the seconds as he commanded, "Starboard-fire! Port-fire! Starboard-fire!" and so, until the last bean had tallied to the last gun of the salute. Oh, it was *great!*

In the afternoon the English troops drilled in front of the Grand Hotel. I was in our admiral's launch, and from the hettaba took in the scene. It was a pleasing one, and when the bands played "God Save the Queen," all the ladies upon the balconies waving flags, handkerchiefs, and parasols, took up the air and sang it.

It was the first time in two years that I had heard a lady's voice.

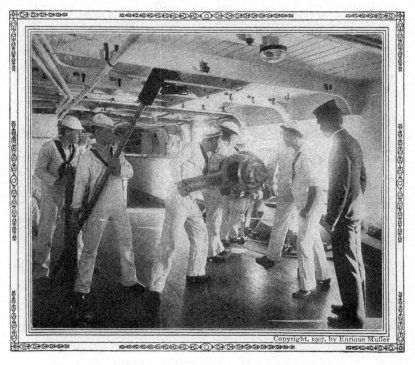

Gun-drill on the *Olympia*.

Chapter XVII

The Day We Celebrate falling upon Sunday, we "made good" the following Monday, and probably never before had a ship's deck undergone such changes. A flume made from sheet-iron started up in the skids, and dipping and bending widened into a big basin on the spar deck, grew narrow again, extending out over the ship's side. It was lined with stones and moss, and set about with countless pots of Japanese ferns, flowers, and shrubs. When the pumps set to work a hidden hose supplied the water; it ran and jumped and sparkled, overflowing the lake, on which sailed a six-foot yacht (a perfect model of the *Defender*), then, trickling into a feathery bamboo forest that completely shut off the ship's rail, fell in a graceful natural waterfall into the bay.

Since 1776 it has been customary for all English men-of-war in foreign ports to go out cruising on the Fourth of July. Our sixty guns proved a panacea for the old grievances; they not only dressed their ships in America's honor, but the crew of *H.M.S. Undaunted* attended our afternoon entertainment. As they came aboard they were each presented with one of the printed programs. And gallantly they pinned to their neckerchiefs the little silk flag that lay between its leaves.

The program went off without a hitch, but I am fain to write it that the number not down was the one to win the laurels.

The fencing contest between Japanese sword masters was over, and the victor was making his salaams to the audience, when one of our blue jackets stepped out and by gesture challenged him again to combat. The vanquished, realizing the purport of his maneuvers, unbuckled his armor and offered it to the seaman, who declined all save the helmet and sword. This he wielded like a ball bat, and in a much shorter time than he had taken to win his laurels the victor was vanquished; and only for the interference of the audience the setting sun would have trailed his last gleam upon a Japanese corpse under the bamboo trees. Oh, it was a glorious day, followed all too soon by one of sadness, for it marked a break in our family.

It was quarters, and Captain Reed, accompanied by a stranger, took the deck. Colors over, he said:

"Captain Gridley, I turn over to you, not only the finest ship that ever rode the seas, but the *finest crew* that ever manned one."

There were tears in his eyes and in his voice, and, what surprised us most of all, a smile benignant lit up his face. It was the first we had ever seen. Was he glad to go, or had the falling of the mantle disclosed the man?

If from my humble station I dare address familiarly one so exalted, I would say, "Captain Gridley, I know your motto," and when I had quoted: "Write me as one that loves his fellow-men," he might not answer, but he would not deny me.

Our Independence
Day Program.

Programme of Afternoon Sports.

Monday July 5th, 1897.
Sports to Start at 12.45 P. M.

Boat Races.

		PRIZES.
CUTTERS .... 12 oars, 2 miles.....Marines vs Firemen		$26.00
CUTTERS ....10 oars, 2 miles.............................		$22.00
WHALE BOATS OR GIGS. 2 miles...........................		26.00
SAMPAN RACE..............................	$3.00 and	$2.00

Deck Sports.

TUG OF WAR... O. S. and Lds. vs C. P. (12 men a side)	...$20.00
MAST HEAD RACE.......................................	$5.00
SWIMMING RACE .... $5.00 and	$3.00
GO AS YOU PLEASE ... (10 minutes)........ $7.00 and	$4.00
CAKE WALK. (In old Virginia Style). 1st prize in the cake, 2nd	$5.00
THREE-LEGGED RACE.................... $5.00 and	$3.00
GREASY POLE.......................................	$5.00
PIE EATING .... $5.00 and	$3.00
HORIZONTAL BAR......................................	$5.00
HIGH JUMPING .... $5.00 and	$3.00
THREAD THE NEEDLE RACE.............................	$5.00
2 BOXING BOUTS....(Winner in each bout to receive $5.00 prize).	

"STAR SPANGLED BANNER."
By the Ship's Company.

A Fencing Contest between Japanese Sword
Masters will be a Special Feature

→ JUDGE AND STARTER. ←
Ensign F. B. Upham.

Day Fire Works at intervals throughout afternoon.
Night Fire Works from 8.45 to 9.45 P. M.

He had been heard to say that the hardest part of a captain's duties is squaring sticks, while he began issuing dinner invitations the first day he took command. Beginning with the first lieutenant, he went through the rank and file of commissioned and non-commissioned officers, and after the boatswain had dined with him he began again at the top, and is keeping the ball in motion.

It is only because of his kindly nature we can forgive him for bringing us back here to Woo-sung, a country so very flat that the only visible undulations in its contour look like bake ovens and prove to be graves; to me at least it is uninviting. And if I have omitted mention of Canton, which is only seventy-five miles up the river from Hong Kong, it is probably because it has been made so familiar by writers, and is so like Shanghai that the only special impression left with me was the one I received when a gang of us were coming out from the Temple of Five Hundred Gods.

We were peaceably going our way when, with out the slightest provocation, a big Chinaman spat at me. I drew back to strike him a well-deserved blow, but was caught and held powerless by my shipmates, who explained, while I struggled, that were I to strike him, not one of us might hope to escape alive. What might have been? Why, *I* might have been the cause of an American-Chinese war.

Have I not read that there are few dogs in China and that the babies never cry? He who wrote it must have made his observations from some European hotel porch. I have seen dogs thicker than on the bench, while the babies who dwell in the floating homes of the Canton

River keep up a wail as incessant as the swish of the tide.

Admiral McNair, desirous of going up to Tientsin, and realizing that the *Olympia* could not navigate the river or canal, took his flag with thirty or forty of our crew on to the *Monocacy*. Poor old side-wheeler with its crew of antiquarians, how proud she was to be a flag-ship, if only for one moon, and how glad we were to leave her after our uneventful trips! There was interest in studying the river life and the diversity of crafts, and my earnest wish is this: "If the dream-man ever brings me anything from China may it be one of her flower boats."

While we were doing Tientsin the boys in Man-o'-war Pool, besides scraping barnacles, had a little excitement of their own. One of the steadiest men on ship one day had occasion to enter the captain's cabin when that gentleman was entertaining an officer from one of our other ships. The stranger recognized him. What he told Captain Gridley we never heard. We know only that the man was put in the brig with double irons. He offered no resistance, merely asking to go on deck for a moment to get something belonging to him. The request granted, he electrified all onlookers by jumping overboard, swimming ashore, climbing over the levee, and escaping altogether and forever. I record this not as a sea yarn, but as a swimmer's record.

The novelty of foreign ports is fast wearing off, it is call here, and call there, then to Mirs Bay for practice or to the Kowloon dry-docks for repairs.

"We are seven." I refer to the Asiatic squadron, and when two or three of us are gathered together in foreign ports it is like meeting friends from home, and one of the greatest temptations that beset the sailorman's path on these occasions is that of borrowing time. For instance, if your shore-leave is for twenty-four hours you are apt to find thirty necessary to the carrying out of your program. Result? The ship sets a monetary reward upon the head of an overtimer, taking it out of the captive's pay. The detective and police forces of Japan reap a nice little revenue from the capture and deliverance on board ship of the American sailor.

So long as Jack keeps in a gang there are none bold enough to interfere, but let him once wander off by himself!

Illustration: Scotty, boatswain's mate of the port gangway, lingering on and on until he was the last of his clan on shore, was finally captured and brought aboard in irons, which the deck officer imperatively demanded to be removed. The moment the left cuff was unlocked Scotty seized it in his right hand, letting fly a blow that all but killed his captor. Poor cop, in addition to his beating, he forfeited his fee, as the law requires irons to be removed before a prisoner goes into a sampan. (A man must have a chance for his life.)

The boys have established a little game with Yokohama's police. Permitting themselves to be taken four or five in a bunch, they walk unironed and take their places in a sampan. When near the ship they capsize the sampan, swim to the gangway, which they mount, and, dripping, deliver themselves, insisting that no reward be paid, as they came of their own volition, and refusing to pay fare, as they were prisoners, not passengers, when they entered the sampan.

One time during some special fête in Tokyo I was in a gang who voted to prolong the stay to the limit.

The limit for conduct, Class Number One, is forty-eight hours, diminishing in duration as one falls from Class One to Class Four. On special occasions, such, for instance, as that of our first visit to Yokohama after the typhoon, we are granted seventy-two hours, but there are other occasions when time is too short and the seaman borrows from the ship. (It *is* a loan simple and pure, for when taking we know just what interest we shall have to pay.)

On these overtime excursions, when funds grow low a tarpaulin muster is taken—that is, every man empties his pocket, giving the contents over to an elected treasurer, who from that moment proceeds to spend it for the benefit of the crowd. When the treasurer sees that his funds have shrunken to a size that will allow only twenty sen to each man, he calls them together, and in a sampan they return generally clean and sober, though not on time.

It is well to understand what liberty means. Say you have been granted forty-eight hours. If you stay fifty you have *broken* your liberty. If you get back in nine days and twenty-three hours you are an overtimer, while if you stay ten days you are a *deserter*, and dare not return. Therefore, once you are an overtimer the duration is kept inside the limit, and is determined by the contents of the tarpaulin or success of the police.

Once more I say, poor police! Sometimes, when matters grow grave, the collecting of stray sailors is given into the hands of the detectives. On such an occasion a crowd of us were walking along Sailor Town, when one of those august personages was recognized with a bunch of arrest warrants sticking out of his pocket. Sam Davis, an Irish-American with a physique like Jim Jeffries, walked up and pulled them out of his pocket, ran them over until he found his own, then in the prettiest of pidgin English asked, "You see this one? This one all e-same me. You likee take me?"

The Jap's knees knocked as he meekly answered, "No, me no want ye."

Then Sam tore the whole bunch into bits.

This same Sam is unique in various ways, one of them being his method of spending his time between enlistments, for Sam is among the ocean-wedded. At the expiration of a term our Uncle gives his sailors three months vacation with pay. Last season, when we were in Nagasaki, Sam got his triennial and proceeded to get rid of the lucre he had hoarded. His first day on shore he spent one hundred dollars. Realizing that this was an extravagance, he counted his money out into piles of fifty dollars each, putting himself on a daily allowance. When night came, if he had not spent the sack he threw all that remained in it to the beggars.

Sam was back on ship long before his three months were up; he said he was afraid the boys would sail away and leave him.

I suppose these reminiscences will be incomplete unless I write something about the marines. What shall it be?

When a little tad I used to count the buttons on my jacket by repeating, "Rich-man, poor-man, beggar-man, thief." Here we read them, "Sailor, soldier, dog, marine," and that it may not look like sailor spite I will tell a little story about the chaplain, who, in exhorting a crew, wound up with the touching peroration:

"Officers have souls to save, sailors have souls to save, yes, even the poor marines have souls to save!"

Chapter XVIII

On the Deep—Adamastor—A Burial at Sea—In a Driftwood Fire

The life of a seaman is not lived entirely in port. When cruising out on the broad ocean we steer clear from the tracks laid for the mail-ships, choosing a pathless waste where there is uninterrupted target range. I should like to write of thirty-seven days out of sight of land, just cruising, and drilling as a long cruise, but when I hear sailormen telling tales of more than a year afloat on an old wind-jammer I am ashamed to mention it, although I cannot leave off wondering where all the blue comes from. Has the ocean drunk from the heavens until they have grown pale, or is the sky merely a mirror of the ocean's sapphire?

In the calmest of weather there are always great blue swells far out at sea, so blue, so free from whitecaps that one requires but slight imagination, by looking through half-closed lids, to see great rolling meadows of gentians. This is where all the pretty little formalities of port life are laid aside the moment the anchor is on deck, the ship's flag and the union jack are folded away, and their staffs taken down, while simultaneously with their lowering an ensign mounts to the gaff and the admirals flag shrinks on the main truck.

It is at sea we get in our hard work, and there is so

much of it that half of the crew (two hundred men) are always on duty.

If for the cruise you are chosen as a helmsman, you are exempt from sea watch, deck work, etc.

It isn't a bit jolly to stand a trick at the wheel: it is two hours on and four hours off, day and night. Not a word dare you speak, and the presence of an officer near by makes a stolen smoke impossible. Were a choice offered I would say, give me a mid-watch aloft in a storm in preference, for there, when the night is cold (although it is not so written in the regulations), a peculiar jerking at a signal halyard tells you that a can of hot coffee is on the way, and when it comes up, you bless it from the fullness of your heart.

For variety at sea, once when we had been practicing with the six-inch guns, and were "securing" for dinner-hour, we saw a monster spouting off our starboard beam. We begged to take a shot at it, and the officer of the deck, recognizing an impromptu target, gave us leave. We fired two shots, and the expression, "a sea of blood," which I had always looked upon as an extravagance of speech, became a reality. When we returned from mess the ocean for a mile surrounding the whale was as red— well, as *red as blood*.

It is during these cruises that we get down to hardtack and salt-horse. The zest of the brine savors everything, and a man no longer eats his meals or goes to "chow," but "scoffs his scouse," and it is the place where the man-o'-war cocktail gets in its deadly.

To be found drunk at sea while on duty is not a matter to make light of, yet serious as it is, I have known Jack Weir stoutly to deny the charge of drunkenness, and to

The derelict in the driftwood fire.

"Far out at sea."

demand audience with the Lieutenant-Commander, of whom he would ask a certificate from "Microbes" to prove that he was drunk.

The harangue ends in a sort of vaudeville "stunt" that delights both officers and men. The doctor comes, feels Jack's pulse, pronounces him drunk, and without further protest the patient goes to the brig.

The eight-inch turret-guns, which we keep like burnished silver in port, we treat to a coating of white lead and tallow at sea. When the weather invites, drills and gun practice are gone through again and again. Neptune forbidding drills, just for the sake of keeping a fellow busy I have often squilgeed and tried to dry the decks when every second wave left them awash fore and aft.

On dark nights sometimes we flash signals upon the clouds, and if one of our own ships sees it, she answers back from miles and miles away.

Often have I been forced to the exertion of my utmost strength in fighting the wind as I struggled aloft, where I would stand pinned to the top mast by the storm.

It is on nights like this that the old salt warns, "Look out for Adamastor," a hideous phantom whose face is scarred by lightning and whose eyes shoot fire. The roaring one hears in the rigging is his awful voice, hissed between blue teeth and lips of black, warning the sailor that the shipwrecked shall be made to deplore their foolhardiness. (Whenever a ship is wrecked, the sailors alone are to blame.)

Adamastor is only one of many sea-spooks firmly believed in. Let the incredulous but smile at a recital of his prowess, the sea-dog will growl, an effectual answer to questioning or doubt. And do you realize, just from association, that even in your unbelief you find yourself looking for him on dark nights when shifting the graveyard watch?

One night I thought surely I had met him, but it turned out to be a flash of lightning so near my face that it blinded me. I told Purdy about it, and he said, "You have seen him, lad. He was batting his eyes at you because you were sleeping on watch."

There are some incidents of the deep sea that a natural shrinking from things unpleasant has caused me to omit. For instance, on our ten days cruise from Chi-fu to Vladivostok, when poor little Coxswain Jimmy died, it was the first burial at sea I had ever witnessed. It was at six bells of the forenoon watch when Pat Murray piped: "A-l-l h-a-n-d-s bury the dead!"

We mustered on the spar-deck, where the starboard gangway ladder lay reversed alongside, revealing a smooth, well-finished, rounded sluice, which I at once suspected of having been so fashioned for a purpose. At its upper end, sewed up in his hammock, with a shot at his feet and the union jack spread over him, our shipmate lay.

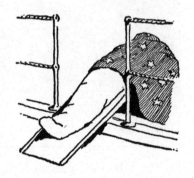

Burial at sea.

With heads uncovered and bowed in solemnity, we listened to the chaplain's prayer, ending with, "We commit thy body to the mighty deep." Then the gang-plank tipped and the body shot from under the union

A derelict—"out on the trackless waste of the Pacific."

jack out into the ocean; three volleys of musketry were fired over the water; the bugler sounded "taps," and the cannon boomed "farewell." (It is the only time a sailor ever goes over the starboard gangway.)

During the service the ship stopped her engines, but it could not have been fifteen minutes from the piping to quarters until all hands were back at their stations and it was all over. (Sometimes I envy the man with a lame memory and no imagination.)

It was in the early dawn of the star watch, when the sea and the sky were our world, that I stood in the yards watching the dawn spreading her rosy path for old Phoebus as he came riding out of the deep. I never tire of the picture; and as I looked, between it and me there arose that which regulation demanded I should report.

"Sail O!" I cried.

"Where away?" from the bridge.

"Three points on the port bow, sir."

"Can you make her out?"

"I think it is a wreck, sir."

It proved to be a derelict, the first I had ever seen, and although I have met many since that day, I can never forget it nor cease to wonder *where* she had sailed from. Generally a boat is sent out with mines and the derelict blown into driftwood.

But this much do I know of my future: whenever I sit by a driftwood fire I shall see that derelict, green with moss like a rotted tree in the forest, nests hanging from her broken spars, and the old hulk rolling and floating aimlessly, monotonously, as the sea-gulls circle about, crooning their lamentations.

CHAPTER XIX

O n entering port we are met by the harbormaster, who conducts us to our berth. As soon as we are anchored or moored, all hands turn to and get things into shipshape. After the national salute, if there is another flag-ship we salute her, and are answered back thirteen guns for our own two stars. It is little short of marvelous how quickly so many things can be accomplished. If it is warm weather the awnings are spread, and when the union jack goes up at the bow we are ready for a season at home. (Have I written it before that the union jack never flies when work is going on, only when the ship is in perfect order, and also when she is at anchor?)

There are many "social functions" held in the cabin and ward-rooms, while the crew, in ways peculiar to themselves, revel in entertainments that are at least unique.

One day, on the bulletin-board there appeared the following

NOTICE:

Casey's Band will give a full-dress concert, forward on the berth-deck, at 6 bells t'night. All hands invited.

145

Nobody went ashore, and six bells found a full house gathered to greet Casey's Band. Their uniforms were oilskins, their instruments the ones discarded by the ship's band for more modern ones.

These instruments had been sent down to the hold, where Purdy was heard to remark, "If they only had mouthpieces they would be as good as new." It was a light task for "Chips" to fashion excellent mouthpieces from empty spools, while to fit a man to each horn was no trouble at all.

Casey, the leader, had played in a band before, and blew a fairly good cornet, and the natural confidence that most seamen possess in their abilities supplied the other necessary talent. Anyway, taken as a "*toot*" they were a success.

To save brainwork in the arranging of a program, they took one of the old ones used by the ship's band. It was great, and when they essayed "Cavalleria Rusticana" the audience rolled upon the deck with laughter—a very triumph of applause.

Casey's Band flourished at the dog-watch for several weeks, fell away piece by piece, finally dying a natural death.

By making a point of returning on board "O.T.C.S.," I have had about all the shore-leave that was coming to me; still I must apologize to my dear Uncle for questioning his judgment, I being of the opinion that *someone* in power is too old to realize how much time ashore is really necessary to satisfy the cravings of Jack Tar.

To break time is so expensive that one can ill afford it, and we are forced either to forswear our heart's craving

Casey's Band.

Adamastor.

or to "jump ship."

There are several ways of going about the latter, the chief requisite in any of them being a marine on guard who is endowed with at least semi-human instincts.

I recall an evening in Yokohama when I was watching for my chance to shinny down the anchor-chain, when the forecastle sentry said, "I'm on to you, Jack, and if you are not out of my sight in five minutes I will run you up." Then, like a gentleman, he turned his back while I proceeded to obey orders.

It is easy enough to crawl through the hawser-hole, clamber down the chain, drop into a sampan and be rowed ashore, but not always so simple a matter to get back, for there is uncertainty about the anchor-watch, and a certainty that an officer will be at the port gangway with the shore-list.

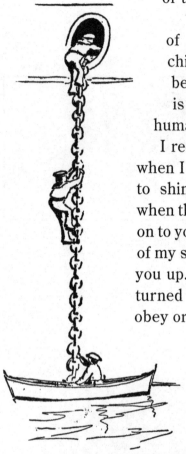

It is easy to crawl through a hawser-hole and clamber down the chain.

If he is new it is easy to borrow a name both to go and to return on, thus many a time have I skipped ship and returned without detection, but there came a day when the port gangway was our only port of entry. Andy Burns was with me, and it was he who proposed that we run a bluff. Accordingly, when the liberty party was coming off we joined them, saluted, and reported, "Returned aboard, sir," and passed on with the bunch. I was hugging myself in delight and picturing a future in diplomatic circles, when the officer-of-the-deck sent for us and said, "Young men, don't think you have fooled anybody, and see to it that you don't attempt this trick again." That man is a brick, and will make a good admiral!

Home was never like this! Nevertheless, we have grown to speak of Yokohama as home. We know every street in her town and every craft in her harbor; we have visited the men-of-war of every nation that floats one, always returning prouder than ever of the *Olympia*. The British tars call her a shipload of guns. They have a battle-ship, the *Powerful*. We look like a steam-launch alongside of her. Her crew numbers more than three times as many as ours, while she carries less than our complement of guns.

Because of a common language it is with the English sailor we engage in shore games. Many boxing matches are "pulled off" between the tars of the United States and its mother country with wavering results.

In boat-racing the eagle has beaten the lion and the unicorn every time, and of the races that are confined to our own squadron, and which take place almost every time we come into port, I am proud to write that the stars are thickening about the Cock of the Station, and that he still roosts on the *Olympia's* yard-arms.

It was in the old days when Lieutenant Sturdy was executive officer, and on one of his regular tours of inspection, that he stopped at the hatch and looked down into the brig. What he saw was about twenty men doing thirty days in the brig. When Lieutenant Sturdy came upon them they were seated in a row, each upon his diddy-box, a well-organized minstrel troupe who good-humoredly accompanied their songs with the rattling of their fetters. At the moment in question two of them who wore only bracelets were doing a double buck-and-wing so dexterously they had won the approbation of the guard, who, leaning his gun against the brig's side, was vigorously working both hands and feet in beating time for the dance.

It hurts me to write the sequel. The poor guard was called up, put into double irons and sent below, where he was denied a position in the troupe. A sailor even in the brig could never stoop to familiar association with a marine!

After dark it is supposed that none but our own boats or those bearing our officers or men will approach the ship. Therefore, when the bridge lookout calls "Boat ahoy!" there can be but one of these answers. If it is Flag-officer: "Flag"

Chief-of-staff, if not in command of the ship: "Fleet"

The captain: "Olympia"

Other commissioned officers: "Aye, aye!"

Other officers: "No, no,"

A sailor or enlisted man: "Halloo!"

Boats not intending to go alongside answer "Passing."

One night the quartermaster reported "Captain coming alongside, sir." To his astonishment, the boat pulled up at the port side and up came Bill Bartley, hopelessly intoxicated. Unlucky Bill! The only shore-leave he ever got was the quarterly twelve hours a man must take willy-nilly, and, as is understood in Bill's case, that he swims for. But this was an offense most serious, he had answered "Olympia," instead of "halloo," and for such a transgression could not bide the "stick," but the very next morning was taken into the skipper's cabin.

Captain Gridley immediately recognized in Bartley a seaman he had known since he himself was a midshipman.

The pros and cons of that heart-to-heart talk can only be guessed at; but Bill, instead of going to the brig, came forth with every offense that was scored against him wiped off the slate and his forfeited pay restored. He was put into the First Conduct Class, where he has remained from that day to this. Bill as a blacksmith, has always been invaluable, but today there is not a soberer, better behaved, man on ship.

I can never think of B. B. without the accompanying subject of swimming; and what jolly times we have, too! There is always a lifeboat out at swimming hour, and the safety born of its proximity has made us fearless and expert. On summer nights we often don our swimming tights underneath our uniforms, and when clear from the ship, strip and jump overboard, swimming and floating until we go ashore at Homoca, where we loll beneath the vines until our clothes overtake us.

Bill Bartley's chevrons.

Then for a sailor's moonlight picnic, often watching the varied water carnivals. One that comes in August,

"The Festival of Departed Spirits," I can never forget, although I shall make no effort to describe it.

We did not carry our luncheon to these picnics, but bought American sandwiches at Japanese booths and washed them down with beer. A prosaic subject that makes a poetic picture. I mean the bottles hidden neck deep in lacquered tubs of cracked ice: the ice catches the glints from the lanterns, and flashes back the amethyst hues of the wistaria.

Chapter XX

Ring out the old,
Ring in the new.

For 1898 has dawned and my "three-years'" enlistment is drawing toward an end.

What a pity that I should have fallen from the log, there have been so many happenings worth relating at the home fireside had I but jotted them down! This brushing together of port and deep-sea incidents is but a poor apology for all that I might have written.

There are men who have lived for years upon the water, sailormen every inch, whom I would not forget if I could.

There is Pat Kelly, master-at-arms and ven-due-master of the lucky-bag, who always announces himself, as he heaves in sight, "Now, here I am, and a-fare-you-well. On the jump from morning till night"; and another Pat, the chief boatswain's mate, as quiet and well-behaved a gentleman as one would ask to meet in civil walks. One day, in his modest manner, he was commanding the lowering of a boat, when a lieutenant, looking on, interposed, "Lower away a little aft, there." Pat Murray paid no attention to the officer, but blew his whistle as a warning to the boat's crew, and in his wonted manner commanded, "Lower away a little *for'ard.*" The men obeyed, and Lieutenant Y., in a burst of temper, unbuckled his sword, and, proffering it to the boatswain's mate said:

"Here, you'd better take my sword."

"Very well," replied Murray, taking off his cap that he might remove the black lanyard from his neck, "You take my whistle."

The lieutenant walked aft as he buckled on his sword, trailing in his wake a volley of exclamations that would have enriched the vocabularies of Seaman McCue or Jack Weir.

Jack Heeny's chevrons.

Jack Heeny, the First Class boatswain's mate, is the very opposite of his chief. He pipes his whistle like a flageolet, and in its returning echoes blends a deep-sea voice that sounds like the voice of a lion at feeding-time in the zoo. There is nothing on earth or sea like his call, "N-o-w, a-l-l-ll you men whose name is on the liberty list, s-t-a-n-d by to go ashore!"

At first I thought some monster of the deep was roaring, but I have learned to understand his every call, even when it is absolutely inarticulate.

By some strange phenomenon two drinks of spirits will completely drown his voice. This submerging of the vocal chords in no manner interferes with his whistle; so the men have learned to *look* when they hear it. Sometimes we see him bracing, with legs wide-spread, his jaws violently working, but not a sound escaping from his lips.

Another boatswain is of the Second Class and belongs on the gun-deck at the port gangway. If there was ever one drop of the milk of human kindness flowing in that man's veins he certainly spilt it in one of the twenty-one shipwrecks he has been in.

And where, oh, where, I ask again and again, do all the rest of these men come from? For more than two years I have been asking it of the blue ocean, and of the stars that shine above it, but they will not answer me. Can it be—? Yes; these men of the deep, from Rear-Admiral McNair down to the lowliest of the marines, are the grown-up children of the kindergarten, public schools, and colleges of our glorious nation. You can find them there in embryo, every one of them. Probably the admiral made his debut in the little log schoolhouse near his father's farm, for, some way, it seems that men get a better start there, for although they are seldom the chosen at the beginning of the race, they most frequently come in on the home-stretch, head and neck ahead of the incubated children of the city.

As to caste in the navy, it knows neither wealth nor family; nor does the decoration on cap or sleeve have the weight it does in the army—every midshipman expecting to be a rear-admiral before he is retired.

In studying the crew, I recalled the words of a great philosopher: "A man is not his father, but himself"; otherwise there would be scattered among our lowly ranks, merchants, doctors, a minister of the gospel, an editor and a bank president; while among the commissioned, where one looks only to find "a gentleman and an officer," it sometimes happens a snob sneaks in.

There is an ensign whose name I need not write, for

I shall never forget it. That fellow has developed the brute instincts in my nature until I can never feel myself a man until I have avenged his insults. Repeatedly he has goaded me beyond human endurance, watching me grow pale with resentment; he once taunted me still further with, "Why don't you strike me?" To have yielded to the temptation would have landed me in the stone frigate, where I must have remained for five years in penal servitude. I thank heaven I was able to restrain myself, but the world is small, and the years of man are reckoned at three score and ten. Some day we shall meet on shore, and whether it be at the court of St. James's, or in the court of the Palace Hotel, I will thrash that little cur until he begs for mercy. When I have done this I can laugh at every other indignity a seaman's life has brought to me.

Three score years and two retires an officer from service. In the full power and pride of a magnificent manhood Rear-Admiral McNair has left us. Soon someone will come to replace him; then the *Baltimore* will return to our relief just as we did to hers. The flag and the band will go with the new admiral back to her, and, rumor says the *Olympia* will return *via* the Suez Canal, calling at the chief ports of the Mediterranean, then to New York under the coach whip of Captain Gridley.

CHAPTER XXI

He came aboard at Nagasaki, dressed all in gray, every snap of his keen black eyes telling that he was not delighted with his berth, and for that matter neither were we, the crew, exultant when we looked to our gallant-mast and saw that we had lost a star. It was *Commodore* Dewey who was succeeding *Rear-Admiral* McNair. McCue timed his sweeping to accompany his cracked voice, and he sang,

> "Hurrah! hurrah! for southern right hurrah!
> Hurrah for the bonnie blue flag, that bears a
>   single star."

But the swallowtail saves it. Oh, the discrimination of flags and pennant! Some day, when I have *nothing to do*, I will go to the flag locker, just around from the ship's library, study them out, and write a descriptive poem about them. A flag that means "yes" at the main truck means "no" on the after gaff. We carry the ensign of every country under the sun, and among our rating flags there are blue fields, with one, two, three, or four white stars, standing respectively for commodore,

157

Commodore Dewey's state-room on the *Olympia.*

rear-admiral, vice-admiral, and admiral. Of the last our navy has had but two;* Farragut and Porter. It will cost another war to restore the office.

Purdy recognized the new-comer on sight; says he cruised the Mediterranean with him when he was a middy, and Scotty says, "Him and me was shipmates with Farragut at New Orleans." These two, with others of the old guard, having approved, we have nothing to do but accept their verdict, and certain it is he can render an admiral's inspection quite as miserable as his predecessor. This through with we started back for Yokohama, making our seventh trip through the Inland Sea.

I have seen it in the rosy bloom of spring; in summer, when the purpling mists from the hills came down and nestled among the pendant wistarias; in autumn, when the rose had deepened into crimson, and the golden kiss of Midas awakened it to unwonted splendor. But on this, my last voyage, I thought it more beautiful than ever before, for the cold winds coming down from the home of eternal snow crisped the air until the halos on the heads of the sailors' guardian angels shone with uncommon radiance.

Some time I am coming here again; coming when I may sleep all day undisturbed in my berth, and lie awake all night upon the deck, watching the stars as they guide the mariner on his way. Or I will loaf all day upon the deck and *sleep all night*. Oh, joy in the thought to sleep again a whole night through!

We were disappointed on entering Yedo Bay not to find the *Baltimore* waiting for us. However, I have still five months to serve, and really I think I prefer this to a

---

*Dewey is the third.

home port, just so I am in California on the twenty-fourth of next June.

What a change! Two weeks after writing the above, weary of waiting for the *Baltimore*, we were returning to Kau-lung to make ready for our home-going. No sooner were we sighted at Hong Kong than every flag in Victoria dropped to half-mast. A signal was given us and we read in consternation: *"United States Battleship* 'Maine' *was blown up in Havana Harbor on February 15, and 266 men killed"*

Before we were at full anchor the American consul was aboard, and the general belief is that the destruction of the *Maine* was the result of Spanish treachery. Nothing authentic nor authoritative has been given out, but I noticed the governor of Hong Kong waived the salute, and that we are not doing any target practice; in other words, we appear to be husbanding our ammunition.

The little commodore has taken matters in hand; he has called all of our squadron to meet here in Hong Kong. He has also bought two ships, which he has provisioned and coaled. As fast as they come in, our ships are run on to the docks and made ready. Should war be declared between the United States and Spain, England, China, and Japan will be neutral, which means we shall be without a berth, our nearest being San Francisco, unless we should go out and capture the Hawaiian Islands, a trick which even for our little *Petrel* would be "like taking candy from the baby."

The little commodore has kept us jumping, and we are ready for whatever may come, and already the men are shouting, *"Remember the* 'Maine'!"

"Coaling."

One morning I saw the ship's painter come out from the commodore's cabin, carrying a long, three-inch wide board painted in various shades of neutral greens or grays. When I asked him what they were for, his answer was both unsatisfactory and inelegant, but the following morning at breakfast the uniform announced throughout the squadron was "old working clothes," and then the boatswain piped, "A-l-l h-a-n-d-s paint ship." That was on the morning of April 19. By noon ships, masts, boats, launches, guns, and everything, had been treated to a coat of "war paint," which, in the United States navy, is dark gray. Unless one has witnessed the painting of a man-of-war it is difficult to imagine how quickly it can be done. There are barrels of paint all mixed and ready before the order is given, and in ten minutes after, the ship is literally manned with painters. The last painting has transformed our beautiful squadron which had gathered together like a

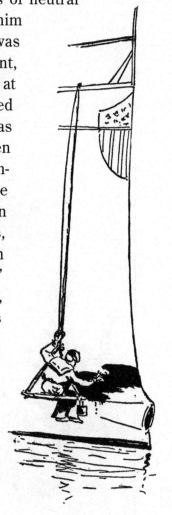

Giving the Olympia her coat of "war-paint."

flock of white swans wearing red favors, into a flock of ugly ducklings sulking upon the water; everything save our spirits and our flags were the color of lead.

As soon as the *Baltimore* reaches Yokohama she will hear the news and hasten to us, and then—?

She came in early one morning, was rushed through coaling and painting, and at the request of the governor of Hong Kong, all hands together sailed away while the men on England's warships cheered us as we passed them.

We are cut off from everybody, aliens in a foreign country, but it can't last long. There is going to be something doing.

It was past noon on the twenty-seventh when our fleet, nine ships all in battle array, was sailing to sea under sealed orders, and with nine crews bursting with expectancy. At five o'clock the *Olympia's* crew was piped to quarters, where we listened to the reading of the following:

Commodore Dewey:

Proceed at once to Manila; engage and destroy the Spanish fleet, when and where you find them.

WM. McKinley, President,
United States of America.

We went mad with joy. The news was signaled from ship to ship, and before we turned in that night a new battle-flag was begun and finished. The placing of the stars proved that we had a representative from each State in the Union. I wrote California and my name on the back of one and sewed it on.

But there was more to do than just the making of

flags. Next morning the order: "Clear for action," was given in earnest, and things we never thought we could exist without went overboard.

From the Chinese-Japanese war we learned that more men were killed by splinters than by shell, and it was rumored the diddy-box must go, but the little Commodore, with the fate of a nation fluttering in his hand, came to our rescue. He said it would be an outrage to take from a man the *only* thing the Navy allowed him to hold sacred, and he asked that we be permitted to stow them below the protective decks—so, here you go! Goodbye, Diddy, until—until we meet again.

CHAPTER XXII

"REMEMBER THE MAINE!"

Remember the *Maine* when great guns roar,
When cannon belch on the hostile shore.
Remember the dead in a sunken ship,
And pass the cry from lip to lip.
Forget the shriek of shot and shell;
Forget for the hour that war is hell.
    For over there beneath the Bay
    Two hundred sailors lie today.

Remember the *Maine* in an alien sea,
That rots with her men for you and me.
Remember the death-cry's mournful note
That rises yet from our sunken boat.
    For souls that rose from out the Bay
    Are leading armies on today.

From "The Bounding Billow."

The council of war was ended and the captains all went silently down our gangway, each entering his own gig; and, as every captain's gig wears a golden arrow on its bow like so many darts shot from the flagship's quiver, they each sought their own target—their own ship.

Everywhere ammunition lay at hand, the guns were loaded, and, although I have hundreds of times answered the order "Cast loose and provide," that night there came a sound in the closing of the breech-blocks that I had never heard before. The click of the steel was gone, and a muffled something that shut in a full charge went through my being. I cannot tell what it was; but I know that every man who fought a gun that day realizes what I mean, and it were impossible to make one who has never heard it understand.

It was news to me that the order "Clear for action!" included the clipping of every man's hair close to his head; the surgeons say hair is as dangerous as cloth in a wound. The climate invited the wearing of "birthday shirts," while for trousers (our only garment) many substituted bathing or boxing trunks.

The surgeons are a jolly good lot of fellows, and an emergency hospital was fitted out in the wardroom for their accommodation. As a gang of us returning from a watch below ran through, a junior surgeon, sitting on the edge of the table, took a cigarette from his mouth long enough to say, "God pity any of you poor devils who come under this," and he flourished an ugly looking knife at us.

I mention this merely as one of many incidents to show the spirit that everywhere prevailed.

From the moment we loaded and trained our guns there was not half the excitement manifested that has accompanied every one of our boat-races, and yet no pen can portray the sensations that alternately raged and slept within our breasts that night.

There were not clouds enough to hide the moon, but

The forwardd deck of the *Olympia*.

we lighted no running-lights, and our stern lights were set in deep funnels that shone *only* astern, and in a feeble glimmer, just sufficient to gage our distance, for we ran in close order.

The flag-ship was in the lead, with Navigator Calkins on the standard compass-stand, listening to the heaving of the lead. "No bottom at ten," or "By the mark seven"— and so the whispers ran through the night, the only sound to break the awful stillness as we picked our way through strange waters; and they were planted thick with deadly mines, which, even as we crept along, would often burst so near that some of our ships got the spray flung by the explosions.

The bells were mute. To the soft swish of the waters the hours dropped off until midnight, when the smoke-stack of the despatch-boat *McCulloch* took fire and gave the enemy our bearings. It was all they needed.

A shell whizzed between the flag-ship and the *Baltimore*, and burst in the water beyond. The *Boston* immediately cut loose with an 8-inch, and the *Petrel* with a 6-inch shell, but it was so dark we could not locate their batteries.

We signaled to the *McCulloch*, "Are you all right?"

The "O.K." she flashed back was the prettiest signal I ever read; it was like a meteor, and when it went out the flagship signaled to the fleet to cease firing.

It was during the starboard watch below that five of us crept away together and told one another things we had never told before. One man gave the stage-name of a well-known actress as that of his mother, and I for the first time owned that my father was a bank president. Addresses were exchanged, and with them, promises that we would write if—well, if anything happened. Then, solemnly laying our hands on our cutlasses, we vowed never to surrender, even though our ship did, and that we would fight as long as there was a glimmer of life left within us. This we swore as the Southern Cross rode out of the water and stood dead ahead on our bow.

It was the first time I had ever seen it, and yet I did not even notice it was beautiful; for I was filled with a sensation I have felt before—felt when in darkness I have groped in a melon-patch where I knew the bulldog slept unchained.

Having run the forts, we swung to the left out of range and slowed down until the ship scarce stirred a ripple on the water. We were commanded to lay by our guns and rest. Was there a man who slept? I know only of what happened in the after-turret with its two 8-inch guns.

The ammunition-hoist that served us both was the dividing-line of the crews: we were eight to a gun, each with a separate and distinct manhood, while as a gun-crew we were the combined vital parts of a steel monster that, gorged with destruction, lay sleeping in darkness.

I knew her as a mother knows her child, and twenty times I took the battle lantern in my hand, and, letting the tiniest of rays peep through its sheath of steel, looked caressingly upon the slumbering gun to see if all was well.

How I longed to waken her, to make her roar, and set all the batteries to screaming! But I must wait, and as I waited, I leaned my head upon her and looked out through her ill-defined porthole into the night.

Just to the right of Corregidor there lay an island. While I looked, something darker than the night traced slender grasses upon its crest, and they grew and grew into leaves of palm that softly fanned the breath of the tropics across the waters.

The breath of the tropics! Like vaporous moon-drops that fall in honey-dew on certain plants, it spread its ooziness over our naked bodies and then it crept into my lungs and tried to smother me in the dark; but the lights of Manila cut through the gloom, so like a familiar picture that I had looked down upon from a hillside in my boyhood that I let go the battle lantern, went wandering away, away, and while I thus groped through the past, zigzags of lightning streaked the sultry night and flashed upon my heart images that had grown dim at sea.

Oh, the faces of my loved ones, never before so beautiful, so dear to me! Fearlessly they filed before the cannon's mouth, each in his or her turn, like the ghosts of Macbeth. I knew it was a phantom of my fancy and yet I wanted to whisper goodbye to them as they passed. I tried to clear my throat, that I might speak, but my voice was gone. Inside my neck a cube of steel incased a ball of something that pressed and pained, but would not be swallowed. I tried again and again, but the pain crept up the sides of my head and out across my shoulders; so I turned away and joined my comrades, where stories and jokes were flying in whispers, but no one spoke again of the past nor of the morrow, and the night dragged its interminable hours along.

The lightning had ceased. From over the hilltops beyond Manila a sob of light like a purpling mist bespoke the resurrection of the sun.

At eight bells—four o'clock in the morning—coffee was served, and once more quarters were sounded.

At a pace of six knots the *Olympia* took the lead, and with every man in the fleet at his post we steamed toward the mouth of the Pasig River, where masts and spires were forming silhouettes against the dawn, which hastened to show us our mistake (they were foreign merchantmen) and to disclose the enemy.

The Spanish squadron, protected by great booms hung with chains, and by lighters of stone and water, lay in line from Sangley Point to Las Pinas, and we swung our course and rode into the fray (for already they were shelling us from the forts) with a leisurely grace of maneuver that we could not have excelled on a Presidential review. And our hearts were threatening to burst from an intensity of desire as we listened to the calling of the ranges, and writhed under the order that passed along the line, *"Hold your fire until the bugle sounds."*

Two bells were striking—it was five o'clock in the morning. The amethyst of an earlier dawn had paled before God's golden crest as it faltered on the hilltops, seemingly listening for the Sabbath bells that for centuries had greeted its coming.

The sun flashed his beams like a benison on the breaking of battle-flags from every flag halyard of America's fleet, and her seamen hurrahed until they were hoarse as they slowly continued the advance and the orders still ran down the line, *"Hold your fire until the bugle sounds,"* and an eleven-inch shell from the city's bastion passed over our quarter-deck. It sounded for all the world like a heavy freight-train going at full speed over a high trestle, but it did no harm. "A range-finder," someone said, and in the silence that followed, every one

Commodore Dewy on the bridge of the *Olympia*.

was thinking what might have been had the projectile sped ten feet lower. And still there was no order to answer this salute!

With cutlass and revolver buckled about his waist every man was at his station. Moments seemed hours. I sat upon the gun-seat repeating to the rhythm of the engine's throb, "Hold your fire—hold your fire—hold your fire until the bugle sounds," while my fingers grew numb upon the spark.

Everywhere shells were flying and mines were bursting, while we, with guns trained to deal death and destruction, were only on parade.

Through the peephole that held the hair-sight of my gun, I saw the Spanish battle-flag break on the enemy's batteries, and we cheered, for they had answered our defiance, and still the orders came faster, "Hold your fire!"

For less than a moment I would close my eyes for rest, for I was gun-pointer. The hair cross in the sight was growing indelible upon my vision, and then in the calling of the ranges I heard distinctly, "Twenty-one hundred yards," and following it like an echo the bugles sounded *"Fire!"*

My eye was on the sight, my hand upon the bulb. That choking thing in my throat fled before the flare of the bugle, and I pressed the spark with as little concern as I was wont to do at target practice.

A quiver ran through every nerve of the ship as we on the pivot guns joining the starboard battery let loose a broadside into the enemy's fleet and left the *Olympia* in a cloud of white smoke that clung to us and enveloped us like a bank of fog.

The great gun, with a recoil of thirty-six inches, had belched her pent-up venom. Riding back on her trunnions, she slid again into battery as No. 2, with crank in hand, stepped out to meet her; and for the first time it occurred to me to count the turning of the crank—one—two—three—four—five—six—seven—eight—nine—ten—eleven turns of the crank made by a stalwart arm, and the breech-block flew open.

Leaning down from my seat, I picked the spent electric primer from the breech and tucked it away in the folds of the neckerchief tied about my head—(a souvenir of the first shot our gun crew fired).

A gentle morning breeze had fanned away the veil of smoke; and, catching a glance through the gun-port, I saw the Spanish ships with masts tilted and lopped away pouring a stream of fire and steel toward us. The water was hissing from their contact, and we cheered the sight while the tub of water beneath the gun-breech turned inky from the swabbing. And up the hoist came fresh charges.

The carriage stopped at the breech. No. 5 shoved in the shell. Another turn, and the first charge of powder stopped to follow the shell; another, and the second charge; and the truck ran back into the ammunition room below as I counted eleven turns of the crank and the breech was again closed upon a full charge. The kid took a fresh primer from his belt, and, adjusting it, signaled with his hand, "Ready!" and again we fired. So perfectly did each man know his part that our division officer had only to sit in the turret and look on.

We were going bow-on toward the enemy when the *Reina Christina,* flag-ship, cut loose her barge, swung away, and came to meet us. We cheered her, and the order came, "Concentrate your fire on the flag-ship." We sent an eight-inch shell from stem to stern, through and through her, and still, like an enraged panther she came at us as though to lash sides and fight us hand to hand with battle-axes, as in the olden Spanish wars.

Our ship had made its turn and the port batteries were manned, when an order came to train the big guns on the forts. We were aching for one more at the *Reina*, but our first shot at the fort dismounted one of her guns, exploded a magazine, and set fire to the arsenal. The strident echoes of the explosion sounded through the din of the combat, and we yelled with delight. Oh, it was *great!* and again I turned and counted eleven twice—when the breech-block opened, and when it closed—again the white veil shut out the picture.

When it lifted our gun was out of training, and I had leisure to look out. I noticed that the admiral's flag was gone from the *Reina Christina* and that boats were pulling away from her, and then I saw the flag break on the foremast of the *Castilla*. It was the signal that withdrew our attack from the *Reina*, and then—great heavens! What was it? We were struck!

Under our own broadsides we had quivered; now we reeled, we careened. Were we sinking? Had they fired us? But the firing was incessant, and the ship, righting herself, was making the second turn. When I had counted eleven twice again it was all forgotten, and we were literally pouring destruction upon the enemy. The *Castilla* was sinking. A madman (Admiral Montejo*), leaving her by

---

*Admiral Patricio Montojo y Pasarón, commander of the Spanish fleet at Manila Bay.

In the fighting-top.

the lee side, returned to the *Reina Christina* with his flag, while a cry arose on our ship, "Here comes a torpedo-boat!"

"Where?"

"There—there—here—no—there—she's gone—no, here she comes the smoke! Where is she? There, rounding the *Castilla!*" and a five-inch shell struck her amidship, broke her back, and she went down, bow and stern sticking out of the water like a bent straw with ends protruding from a goblet. Then, while I watched a tattooed fly undulating with the brawny muscles on the back of No. 4 of the port gun, I twice again counted eleven when a second torpedo-boat, undaunted or maddened by the fate of its sister, came at us, and we drove her back and beached her.

Slowly we advanced upon our enemy; gallantly they came to meet us. The destruction we were dealing grew momentarily more visible, and when the newness of battle passed (as it does in an in conceivably short time), I began to wonder what they had been doing to us. When I had counted eleven twice again and our gun could no longer be brought to bear upon the enemy, I nerved myself to look into the dead faces of my shipmates. Going up out of the turret, I ran along the sun-scorched sanded decks and when I had made the round I thought I must be dreaming, *for every man was fighting at his post!*

I stopped to watch the onset—just as a projectile struck and burst against our aft turret. It made a dent like the concave side of a washbowl in her armor-plate. A warm stream trickled down my leg as I felt the ship turning, and returned to my gun just as the bugle sounded, *"Cease Firing!"* Someone in crossing the

Admiral Dewy on the after-bridge of the *Olympia*.

bridge had remarked that they (the enemy) must have ammunition to burn.

In the confusion of noises only one word, "Ammunition," caught an ear, and we ceased firing and all steamed out into the middle of the bay to inventory shells—and incidentally to breakfast.

I found time to pick out a bit of steel and another of shin-bone, where I had felt the warm blood, and I bound it up without reporting to the sick-bay. (I never felt a pain until three days later, and then I was quite unable to stand upon the injured leg).

Another among the *Olympia's* wounded (if I dare to call my scratch a wound) was Jack Heeney, the bo's'n's mate. Watching the battle with his hand resting upon a gun-shield, he had three fingers shot away. Jack already wears five enlistment-stripes, and while his hand was being dressed he anxiously inquired if the loss of his fingers would debar him from future enlistment. Not a bit of it! It only set the seal of battle upon him, and Jack is good to pipe quarters for half a century to come.

The Spaniards evidently thought we had gone out to bury our dead, and while they thought us thus engaged, the batteries on Cavite kept up an incessant firing; but the range was too long; we were never safer in our lives; and after there had been a conference of commanders on the *Olympia's* quarter-deck, and each had gone back to his own ship to report that not a man had been killed in the engagement, the Asiatic squadron for the moment was like the mad-houses of the world turned loose. When reason returned, again our battle-cry, *"Remember the Maine!"* rent the air, and we returned with vigor to the fray.

We fought the enemy's line, passing five times up and

down its length of ships and forts, cutting our path like a figure 8 (and all the time the navigator was sounding). Whenever our ships would meet on maneuver we would wildly cheer each other, although there was not a sound to our voices, for it was lost in the din of the combat.

Someone was heard to ask in all seriousness, "I wonder if they will report this racket in the San Francisco papers?" Of course they will, but I am wondering *who* can tell the tale? What words can paint it? Can the pen tell how men go down in battle?

As we fought in line I saw on the *Mindanao's* deck a creature in the full flush and vigor of life, silhouetted against the sky. A Yankee shell struck him in the breast. It was like a rifle-ball hitting a blue jay.

I saw boats freighted with wounded men go over the sides of sinking ships; but they flaunted Spain's flag defiantly at us and we shelled them under; I saw men clinging to spars and floating in with the tide, and we shot them to death. I saw tongues of fire licking up the decks of the doomed vessels. These are but a few of the horrors I saw, and oh, I heard such noises! The dull boom of the big guns and the spiteful snapping of our main batteries mingled with the clatter of musketry.

Ah, here is the place to say just one word for the poor marines, to record their excuse for living. What could we have done without them? They were our sharp-shooters, cracking rifles through loopholes and sponsons, aiming for gunners on the enemy's ships. They were also our line of communication, calling ranges, and carrying orders that the bugle could not make heard.

And while we on deck were seeing these things, what were the "black-gang" doing?

Down there underneath the water, in a furnace-room that only Dante could portray, they heard the din and felt the shock of battle. They could not see, but counted the times we were struck (the *Olympia* received thirteen hits all told), and they stood at their posts as though out on a cruise, and ever and anon in the hushes a voice would call up through a ventilator or a hoist, "How are you making it?" An answer like "Just sunk another torpedo-boat," or "They have abandoned the *Reina Christina,* and she is all afire," would drive them wild with a joy they would make manifest by beating upon the furnace-doors with their shovels.

When someone writes of all these things I hope he will not omit mention even of the "galley-hatch gang," they who long ago filed the hinge-screws off the alcohol chest until its lock became a howling joke, for with the ringers the screws could be removed and in the watches of the night its spirits let out.

However, the night before the battle, after the decks were cleared, to a man the "old guard" rallied about their standard, vociferously declaring, "No Dutch courage for us; we will fight a sober battle." Then, with something of the air that characterizes a burial at sea, they slid the chest overboard.

It was in the very excitement of war, while we were out beyond the reach of the enemy's shells, that I felt impressed as never before with the perfect workings of the human, as well as of the mechanical, parts of a man-of-war. While we breakfasted, Bill Bartley was securing a piece of sheet-iron over a hole a Spanish shell had put in our side, and, lest the enemy on our return might gloat over the sight of our bandaged wound, it was even painted before we went back to complete the destruction we had begun.

I do not believe that one half of the horrors of that day can ever be told; and for deeds of courage and daring—on our own ship, in the hottest of the fight, a cleaning-stick broke inside one of the main batteries guns, and it had to be trained in, in order to poke the broken bits out: it was its officer who went outside of the sponson to do the deed, although his command could have sent any man from his crew, and he would never have been thought a shirk or a coward. History writes more about the life and doings of one monarch than of all his subjects, but that is no reason why I, in this my private journal, should not jot down these simple facts about people in lowly station.

Before high noon a white flag hung from the shears on Cavite's wall, and an hour later, when Admiral Montejo, under a similar flag, came on board, he would have parleyed with the little Commodore; but Dewey demanded stoutly:

"Do you surrender?"

"Conditionally," was the answer. "Our cap-i-tan he die, he speaka fighty—fighty for Spain."

"It's either surrender—or fight!" exclaimed Dewey; and Montejo, bowing with the air of a cavalier of old, said, "I surrender."

We were a sorry-looking lot to salute our colors when they broke where the flag of truce had hung. Our faces, begrimed with the smoke of battle, ran rivulets (born of the atmosphere) that, coursing down our cheeks, mingled with the saltpeter eating them into stinging furrows.

"We cheered them as they sank."

But the day did not end with the battle; that evening we pulled two whale boats ashore at Cavite. Only our doctors and an officer landed, but I am glad to have been one to sit in the boat and look upon the picture. It was not unlike those I have seen of the Landing of Columbus. As we pulled shoreward, people wearing long robes came to meet us, and when our officers landed, priests and nuns knelt at their feet upon the beach, beseeching them for mercy. Some of them spoke fair English, yet it was with difficulty they were made to understand that our doctors had gone to them with only one intent—to care for their wounded. The following morning, when we went ashore to bury their dead, we sent for the Spaniards to come and identify them, that they might mark and later claim their own. Only a few came. The Spaniard can reason only from his own standard, and undoubtedly suspected treachery on our part.

Many and varied have been the tasks I have encountered; but to actually assist in the burial of the enemy—that was the climax. It was not a funeral where muffled drum and the perfume of sweet flowers add to the solemnity while it takes away from death some of its sting.

They lay like wreckage upon the beach, washed in from the sunken, burning ships. Does the dead enemy rate any honor? They were one by one (when not beyond handling) stood upon their heads, not in derision, but as a precautionary means of preventing the burial of treasure. Pictures, coins, and rosaries rained upon the shore, and after this final preparation for rest they were placed side by side, hundreds in a row, in the trenches we had dug in the sands above the wash of the tide. Then in the night the wild hogs came, rooting the mangled corpses out of their graves, and we had to do it all over again—do it under the glare of a tropical sun, or in the fury of a tropical thunderstorm. Ugh!

"What was it like, that battle?" do you ask?

The thunders of heaven would have been lost in its din. It was fierce and fast, like the rolling of all the drums in the world, or like bolts of heavy sailcloth torn into shreds by the wind.

What a picture it would make—that battle, the last of the Spanish fleet, the *Don Antonio de Ulloa*. She fought, sinking a foot a minute. Gun after gun went under, and when the last onset was made, only her bow gun remained. Its crew, waist deep in water, fought as though victory were crowning them. It was theirs to fire the last gun upon that eventful day, and we cheered them as they sank.

These are the things men will write about, but memory alone can paint a picture so terrible that the moon, that old night-watch of the universe, hid behind friendly vapors that she might not see the embers of war as they glared through the port-holes and sponsons of half-sunken ships, while ever and anon exploding magazines would tear the waters, and livid flames of yellow and of red flaunted above all that was left of Spain's wreckage.

Surely Wellington was a Solomon when he wrote:

"Nothing except a battle lost, can be half so melancholy as a battle won."

Chapter XXIII

Uncle Sam knows a prize when he draws one; since the tenth of May our main truck again flaunts two stars. Promises of a sword for our gallant hero and of medals for us have been made by Congress, while what we need more than trophies—ammunition and reinforcements—are on the way.

Since the burial of Adam, sailors have been averse to soldiers work, but we have been forced beautifully down to it, and it has brought new experiences into our lives. Think of sailors taking a piano and carrying it for three miles after hoisting it over a stone wall! When we had landed it in shipshape at the water's edge, one of our officers came along and said, "Good! We will have it in our ward-room."

In the ward-room! Not on your life! He was no sooner out of sight than the souvenir battle-axes we were bearing were wielded with a vim that reduced an upright Steinway to a condition that Frank May would have scorned as kindling for the galley-fire.

Frank May! I'll never forget him. He is the fellow who ate Rough on Rats over in Yokohama, and he is still at his post in the galley, and still as regularly as Saturday comes around he goes through a stunt that, only for the seriousness of his mien, would be truly ludicrous. Old Frank goes to the armory and gets a rifle loaded with a blank cartridge, then, like a sentry on duty, marches down the deck and into the galley, where with mumbling and muttering he shoots into the galley's smoke-stack, ostensibly to clear it of soot; but the exultant "There, you black blankety blank, how do you like that?" which invariably closes the scene is at least circumstantial evidence that he has again shot "Charley Noble."

But back to the piano: its destruction engendered much feeling, but as the real name of its acquisition could only be spelled l-o-o-t, there was no complaint entered by the officer who would have appropriated it, and the sailormen's disappointment was solaced by Chaplain Father Reamy,* who bought a piano and presented it to the gun-deck. That priest is truly paving himself a path to heaven by deeds of generosity. Every year he spends more than his pay on amusement for the boys.

In the very rush of the Curio Vintage, after going through the different stages of gathering and casting away for better fruits, twenty of us clubbed together, and by our combined efforts succeeded in getting a dandy little three-inch field-piece on board, intending to raffle it, that one out of the score might carry home with him a souvenir worth while. But the powers that rule have taken it, and will present it with *their* compliments to our godmother the City of Olympia. *Bah!*

And we are bearing these indignities on short rations—government straight—which in the present instance means hardtack so full of weevil that it would

---

*Father William Henry Reaney (1863-1915) was chaplain aboard the *Olympia* beginning shortly after the Battle of Manila Bay.

The signal bridge of the *Olympia*.

be an insult to the canine race to substitute it for puppy biscuit!

Uncle Sam is not doing it with malicious intent. This war came on suddenly, and we were completely cut off from fresh supplies while in Mirs Bay, and it really can't very well be helped. I recall one morning when our supplies had run so low that the cook of Mess No. 3 threw a pair of boxing-gloves and some dumb-bells at us as he had nothing else to serve with our coffee. It was when we were reduced to this, and before we had grown to look upon a banana and a cigarette as a Philippine breakfast, that Sir Edward Chichester, the British admiral, signaled to us, "Send your boats alongside for fresh provisions." The laws of neutrality kept us from accepting this offer, but whenever we have occasion to go alongside the British ships in our boats, when our officers are calling, the English sailors invariably pass us out supplies.

There is a bounteous crop of cocoanuts and mangoes growing inside the Navy Yard, and we have learned to eat the former in a semi-liquid state. It carries me back to the days when I ate raw eggs, not because I liked them, but because it was one way of showing my masculine superiority over my sister.

A taste for mangoes is an acquired one, and although realizing there is only one place where they could be eaten with any degree of decency—that is, in a bathtub—I am really fond of them.

We are cautioned to drink no water ashore, and with a guard at the gate how is Jack expected to quench his thirst?

German export is cheaper here by the bottle than by the schooner at home, but is much more difficult to get.

"Eeny-meeny-miny-mo, Catch-a-sailor-by-the-toe; If-he-hollers-let-him-go- O.U.T. *out*."

The second *out* commissioned me one of three who were to go out and bring in a sackful of bottles.

From the ship we had marked a little cove in the wall of Cavite's fortification, and we chose it as probably available for an exit.

Seamen are good climbers. Reaching the top, we picked a loose stone from the wall and dropped it outside. A dull, echoless thud confirmed our hopes: it was above the waterline, high and dry. It is immaterial who jumped first, but simultaneously we grasped the situation: our bared feet had struck neither sand nor stone, but dead bodies, over which we ran and stumbled through a darkness that at intervals yielded to flashes of lightning revealing the garish eyes of dead men leering at us.

Probably on the day of the battle they were wounded and brought to this little haven of refuge, and later left to die.

We got the beer and were obliged to return as we had gone, it being the only place where a latch-string hung out for us. Before returning, however, we thoroughly discussed the question whether we should report our discovery. For two excellent reasons we decided to leave the whole matter to Time. Already we have noticed crows circling above that part of the wall, and some day (I hope it may be after we are gone) someone will find human skeletons bleaching there in the sun.

It is part of war's destruction, "When unable to capture, spike your enemy's guns." The port at Cavite was equipped with a battery of the latest improved Krupp cannon, every one of which we wound with a bandage of guncotton. Gun-cotton looks just like cube sugar strung on copper wire. When each gun had a string of it around its middle we switched on the current and the deed was done. They were effectually choked, resembling long rolls of butter that had been grasped between the thumb and finger, leaving an encircling depression. Of course it was a shame and a pity, just as it was a pity and a shame to treat the *Mindanao* as we did.

She was a beautiful transport, fresh from Spain, her cargo still aboard, and during the battle she had been run up on the shoals off Las Pines and abandoned. That very day, before the sun had set, as if our engines were playing "Behold El Capitan!" we steamed out and our for-'ard turrets sent two 8-inch shells full length, clean through and through her, then whirled majestically and repeated the salute from our aft turrets.

In the morning she was still there, and we sent the little *Concord* out to set her on fire. She burned for a week, and I never looked toward her devouring flames without wondering how much provision they were consuming; but we are obeying orders. They distinctly read, *"Engage and destroy."*

Among the many escapades ashore there is the one that canonized Connelly a martyr, and that will not be written in "The Bounding Billow" (for there it would be given away, while here it remains a secret).

Doing garrison duty in the yard, a consuming thirst drove a gang of us out in search of liquid refreshment, and as we were scurrying back with our prize, under the first darkness of the night, an officer, who was carrying singly and unaided a heavier "load" than we were packing for the crowd, discovered us and called, "Halt!" Too well we knew what the obeying of that order would bring us, and, realizing that we were not to be recognized, took to our legs. To our astonishment the valiant officer fired two shots after us. One of them hit Connelly in the leg, and that's what made him a martyr. It was a nasty wound. His shipmates dressed it and antiseptically bandaged it. They performed all of his tasks that it is possible for one man to do for another, and although at times the fellow suffered intensely, he was always at muster, and never with a telltale limp.

The other side of the page is this: The scrub who fired at us followed far enough to find a trail of blood on the cement pavement. Then, going out to the ship, he warned them in the sickbay and dispensary to look out for a man who would come in to report a shot in the leg. Unquestionably he felt valorous until the admiral got after him. I hear he roasted him brown. "Would you shoot your own men in time of war?" he asked, then showed him the chances he was taking; for these are the days when every man, from the admiral down, wears a 38-caliber Colt at his side.

Long, long ago, in the days when the sea was so new to me that I wrote of nothing else, there came an incident that, in looking backward, looms up as one of the funniest of my varied experiences.

I was working in a groove that brought me every morning early on the quarterdeck to polish the brass rims of the airports to the captain's cabin. One morning when I came, Smithy was there before me, quaffing nectar from a crystal decanter. He held it toward me, saying, "Come on, Jack, take a drink of your Uncle's best." And so I did, and so we both continued to do every morning that Captain Reed left it within our reach through the porthole. But as all things come to him who waits, Langly, on whom we had blown our scented breath and mysteriously intimated to him that we owned a barrel of the stuff but were not giving any away, looked over from the superstructure deck and caught us in the act. Then the jig was up. The following morning Langly was first at the hole. When we came in sight he was standing with his arm thrust inside the port-hole, and he had turned so pale that I thought he was going to faint at sight of us; but in a twinkling we all knew that Captain Reed had set a trap; an orderly was holding Langly's arm as in a vise, and he spent many days in the brig doing time for the whisky Smithy and I had drunk.

There is a two-hundred-years' accumulation of cannon in the Navy Yard. Long and short, great and small, they are piled like cordwood and strung out like fence-rails. Some of them are so elaborately carved they would make handsome ornaments for home parks and museums.

Poor sailors of Spain! It was not from lack of war's appliances that they were vanquished. It is told of them that when they went to their guns to fire, they actually flinched, just from the strangeness of the act, while every hour of drill we have gone through, and every pound of powder we have burned, has demonstrated beyond a proposition that Uncle Sam has been casting his bread upon the waters.

Perhaps we may have another scrap, one not down on the program, for we have a leader who is not going to wait even for an order from Washington if an emergency

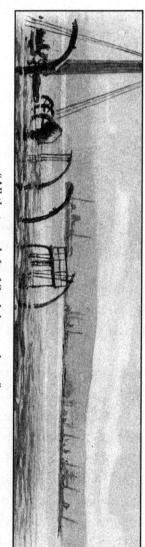

"All that was left of Spain's wreckage".

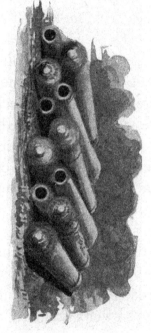

Old Spanish cannon.

arises, and it looks as though that part of Germany which is floating about here were looking for trouble. They are up to all kinds of annoyances, even having gone so far as to turn their searchlights upon our boats at night, for no other comprehensible reason than that of disclosing us to our enemy. Dewey got a mad on the other day and formally sent his compliments to Admiral von Diederichs, with the message that he was "getting altogether too active." The square-head took the hint and piped down.

While men have come and men have gone, I still hang my hammock on hook No. 2149, which is in the first row aft in the starboard gangway on the gun-deck. As all greetings and farewells are spoken at the starboard gangway, I have listened to much chit-chat between our admiral and visiting officers. Once when a German captain came to confer with him his answer was, "It takes an *admiral* to talk with me." Bully for Dewey!

I have grown well acquainted (by sight) with Aguinaldo, the insurgent general, who has be come a frequent visitor on board. In appearance he resembles a small mulatto boy playing soldier with a man's sword dragging at his heels. But it is not for me to criticize his appearance, for it was he who presented us with twenty bullocks, which gave rise to the question of ways and means for converting them into beef.

Tom Reed, a butcher by trade before he came to sea, got the job and called for assistants. I begged, and he let me in on it. When the officer-of-the-deck asked me how long I had worked at the butcher trade I unblushingly answered, "Four years." I think I detected a smile, but he detached me with the killing party ashore, where Tom thought it funny to make me shoot all twenty. It was like murder. I felt no compunction when mowing down human beings with an 8-inch gun, but this butcher business was sickening despite the fact that it served us the first fresh meat we have had here.

Would it be discourteous to remark that the tropics raise better fruit than beef?

Yesterday morning on wakening I immediately recalled that it was the twenty-fourth of June. Taking some extra pains in my dressing, before quarters, I went to the mast, saluted, and said, "I beg to report the expiration of my enlistment, sir."

"Do you want to ship over?"

As I answered in the negative, the conversation abruptly ended. I must have been vaguely expecting they would offer me command of the captured *Callao* if I would only stay.

The captured *Callao!* She came in two weeks after the battle wholly ignorant of the fate of the *Maine*, and came to only after three shots had crossed her bow and the top of her mainmast carried away. Of all the lightning changes I have ever known, that of the *Callao* "takes the cake! "At eight o'clock one morning she was a Spanish gunboat; before ten the Stars and Stripes floated from her stern and a skeleton crew of U.S. seamen were established aboard her.

I shall never forget how the tears rolled down her captain's cheeks when, in answer to his question, "Where is the Spanish fleet?" a finger indicated its shattered hulks and spars sticking out of the water. Slowly it all dawned upon him, and he replied, "Then I suppose I am a prisoner," and surrendered.

Before quitting the ship Dewey caused him to pay off his men from the revenues he had collected, knowing that otherwise they would never get their wages. He then paroled him with his crew, sending them with an escort through our lines. It is reported that he has been shot by his countrymen for not fighting his ship.

What was I saying about remaining? Am I not enlisted for three years, not to exceed five? I would not leave now if I could, but I shall be glad when the soldiers come.

Chapter XXIV

Doing picket duty on the wall, I saw a Spaniard rise out of a trench, sight down the barrel of his Mauser and aim directly at me. Dropping behind, I laid my cap on top of the wall and stepped aside just in time to hear a bullet whizz above my cap. In quick succession two more followed, each a little nearer to the target. Then, remembering orders, I knew it was my turn. I fired only once. It was not answered, so I put on my cap and got back on the wall, but did not go to look inside the trench. I did not want to.

The climate of Hawaii is cool and balmy compared with this. Our scant raiment clings to our bodies like sticky fly-paper to Bill Nye's cat*. To go in swimming would be like throwing shark bait into the surf.

Heretofore when in port during the summer months, each man has paid ten cents a month over to the Second Class master-at-arms. At all times it is he who keeps the scuttle-butt filled with distilled water. With this small tax he buys ice, which is delivered from the shore, and we

---

*Edgar Wilson "Bill" Nye (1850-1896), an American journalist, well known at the time for a humorous essay describing an unfortunate cat and its battle with a sheet of fly-paper.

have iced drinking water. But here, where, of all places we need it most, it is not to be bought.

The ship's converters grind day and night, and the clinking of glasses in the wardroom and on the quarter-deck makes me feel like the rich man in Hades.

An idea! I am not a frequent attendant at church, but if the sky pilot, like Casey's band, would declare himself from the bulletin board, announcing that he would preach a sermon taken from St. Luke, the sixteenth chapter and twenty-fifth verse: "But Abraham said, Son, remember that thou in thy lifetime receivedst thy good things, and likewise Lazarus evil things; but now he is comforted, and thou art tormented." I believe there would not be standing-room for the congregation, and am inclined still further to believe that at least the ice now wasted after cooling glasses for cocktails might be husbanded and put into the scuttle-butt.

I verily believe we could not live were it not for the water monkeys we are forced to make. A string soaked in kerosene is tied about a bottle's neck, set fire to, and while burning thrust into water. It makes a cut as keen and smooth as a diamond. This neck, or mouthpiece, is sewed into one corner of a canvas bag that will contain about two gallons. The one I pull from hangs in the aft turret No. 1. The evaporation through the mesh of the canvas cools the water to a degree, and from the glass neck we all drink, the man emptying it being the one to take it to the scuttle-butt and replenish.

Thunder and lightning! Is it like unto battle, or is battle like a thunderstorm? Though unable to decide, I readily recall a night when we were cruising about, just outside

Manila Bay, I stood in the yards of the mainmast in the darkness of Erebus. I felt as if the world were an eggshell and our ship the only thing in that world. Then, from away off in the great, unfathomable universe, a peal of thunder would split the shell, letting in a chain of jagged lightning just where the sky and water met.

On one of these little cruises the watch aloft one morning reported "Water-spout ahoy!" It was the familiar old picture out of the geography. The quartermaster said, "You may never see an other, boys. Take a shot at it." A single shot from a six-pounder broke it into a spray that, mingling with the waves, rolled peacefully on.

On the morning of the battle (try as I may, it seems I cannot get away from that day) Captain Gridley was so ill that the little commodore offered to excuse him from duty; but, gallantly, as is characteristic of the man, he replied, "Thank you, Commodore Dewey, but she is my ship and I will fight her." And he did, although, figuratively speaking, he was a dead man before he went on the bridge, and days had strung themselves into but

"Water-spout ahoy!"

few weeks when he was ordered home on sick leave. He came up out of his cabin dressed in civilian clothes and was met by the rear-admiral, who extended him a most cordial hand. A look of troubled disappointment flitted across the captain's brow, but vanished when he stepped to the head of the gangway and, looking over, saw, not the launch, but *a twelve-oared cutter manned entirely by officers of the Olympia.* There were men in that boat who had not pulled a stroke for a quarter of a century.

Old Glory was at the stern and a captain's silken coach-whip at the bow; and when Captain Gridley, beloved alike by officers and men, entered the boat, it was up oars, and all that, just as though they were common sailors who were to row him over to the *Zafiro.* When he sat down upon the handsome boat-cloth that was spread for him, he bowed his head, and his hands hid his face as First-Lieutenant Reese, acting coxswain, ordered, "Shove off; out oars; give away!"

Later in the day the lookout on the bridge reported, "*Zafiro* under way, sir," and the deck officer passed on the word until a little twitter from Pat Murray's pipe brought all the other bo's'ns around him, and in concert they sang out, "Stand by to man the rigging!"

Not the *Olympia*, alone, but every other ship in the squadron dressed and manned, and the last we ever saw of our dear captain he was sitting on a chair out on the *Zafiro's* quarter-deck, apparently "listening to the old band play." A week later a cablegram told us that he never reached home, having died on the fifth of June on board the *Coptic.* The grief that filled our hearts abated not, even when the prescribed time for mourning had passed and the flags were released from half-mast.

There is another we miss; but it was but the shifting of officers, which is like unto the shifting of the sands on the shore, that took Lieutenant Delano from us. The last we saw of him, he stood at the stern of the launch, dandling in his hand a fob that hung from a gold watch (a parting gift from the crew) while the band lustily played "Nancy Lee." We loved that man, and feel that had he been lieutenant commander on the first of May, the men who were taken from the brig to fight for their flag (I was not one of them) would never have been sent back to serve out their sentence after the battle, and for the credit of our navy I am glad that it will not be written in our history, and am already half ashamed that I have written it even in this, the chronicles of a diddy-box; but I cease to blush for this as I glow with pride in making note that since the battle not an hour's drill have we done. The admiral says we have proved that we do not need it.

While there are always ground-swells off Cavite, sometimes they grow heavier than at others. It was when they were doing their worst that I lay under the awning in the storm sheets of the admiral's launch, on duty during dinner-hour. She was riding tied to the boom, and I doing nothing but swelter and wait my turn for chow, when I heard a voice calling, "In the barge, there!"

The admiral's launch.

"Aye, aye, sir."

"You're adrift."

I came to, started the engine, and tried to steer back to the ship, but a squall had suddenly come up, and I could not manage her. The orders shouted from the bridge grew indistinct, then inaudible, and I could hear nothing but the elements. For two hours I worked with that launch, climbing back and forth over the thwarts, firing or working her rudder, as she pitched and rolled, frequently carrying me dangerously near the enemy's line. The glasses were upon me, and finally realizing the futility of my attempts to get back to the ship, they signaled to me, "Go ashore." I fired her well up and let her go. As I drew near the landing I steered from casco to casco, striking sidelong blows that set them dancing on the water as they retarded my speed, and then I finally achieved a landing. Filled with pride at my success as a mariner and a navigator, I raked the fire all out and tied her up. She was safe and sound and I knew it. I was indeed weary, having, single-handed and alone, in the face of a tropical squall, performed the task of five men.

To me, the feat looked worth a glass of beer, and I went after it, not knowing that simultaneously with signaling me to go ashore, a whaleboat had started after me, carrying the remainder of the launch's crew; but I was soon to know that they reached the launch before I got back to it, the consequence being that instead of a medal in commemoration of a brave and daring deed I got five days in the brig on bread and water. However, having long since grown callous to these little courtesies, I embraced the opportunity to have tattooed—not a star upon my forehead; but when my earthly cruise shall end and my tired hands lay folded upon my breast, they will rest upon crossed cannon wrapped in the Stars and Stripes; while the American eagle, holding in his beak a banner with the inscription, "Manila, May 1, 1898," will hover above a bursting shell through whose fire and smoke rides the glorious United States Flag-ship *Olympia.*

When I walk with myself, I talk with myself, and myself says unto me, "Jack, if you were to pass a sentence of revenge upon your worst enemy, and you wanted to inflict the greatest torture your mind could conceive, what would it be?" Unhesitatingly I answer, "Deprive him of sleep."

The action of battle is inspiring. A typhoon with all its terror gives you a struggle for your life. But since the battle, with doing garrison duty on shore in addition to double watches on ship, I have come from the lookout, fixing my eyes six feet ahead of me where I was to drop for my rest, when it seemed absolutely that *I could not live* until I reached the spot.

Papers from the States show that this war is giving birth to heroes, and the sailormen of the Asiatic Squadron, if they might have a voice, would beg to say that Navigator Calkins should be known to all Americans as The Path-finder into Manila.

CHAPTER XXV

JUNE 30TH—JULY 16TH—GENERAL MERRITT—AUGUST 14TH—
A TARPAULIN MUSTER

On June 30th the *Charlie,* accompanied by three troop-ships, arrived. It relieved us from garrison duty, but the manning of the *Nansen* and *Zafiro* before we left Hong Kong, together with skeleton crews for the captured *Callao* and the launches we are using for river service, leaves us short-handed on all the ships; but for a' that on the eighth of July the *Concord* and *Raleigh* had a picnic in Subig Bay, and remained in possession of Isle Grande, near Manila.

On the sixteenth a cold-storage ship from Australia came in with a handsome cargo, which the admiral bought on sight. It was the first fit beef we have eaten since leaving San Francisco (all through the Orient they kill a species of carabao or water-buffalo for beef), and while we were regaling ourselves on the fruit of our good fortune the *China* arrived with naval reinforcements.

It was a relief that brought with it a tightening of discipline. Few boats have returned from shore without bringing their complement of battle spoils from Cavite, their accumulation gradually changing the appearance of our decks into those of pleasure yachts, until one morning there came an order that cleared ship and left the bay afloat with rocking-chairs, sofas, and gilt-framed saints.

It was soon like old times, even the brig waxing into renewed favor, until Microbes (ever humane) diagnosed it as unhealthy and unfit for use in this climate. Microbes did his part, but *someone* saw the alternative: put the prisoners in double irons, and chained them promiscuously about the decks. One could not keep from laughing, it was so suggestive of a human kennel.

In coming here we were unable to bring our laundrymen from China or Japan, but the washing problem solved itself in a most unexpected and satisfactory manner.

In the storehouses of Cavite there are thousands of white sailor suits, which we confiscate at will, wearing them until soiled, then casting them adrift for a fresh suit. The cork helmets, too, we have adopted, finding them for comfort's sake a vast improvement on our own headgear for this climate. The most complimentary greeting exchanged now on shore is: "Halloo, is that you? I thought it was Stanley in Africa."

On the twenty-fifth, General Merritt came in on the *Newport*, and on the thirty-first, McArthur's reinforcements reached Cavite. Then followed councils of war; the officers of the army and of the navy meeting on board the *Olympia* to discuss grave matters, which culminated on August 7th, when Admiral Dewey and General Merritt jointly demanded the surrender of Manila. It was refused, and once more we cleared for action and got ready to cast loose and provide.

On the morning of August 14th, the admiral announced that unless the Spanish authorities laid down their arms

The First Nebraska marching up the beach toward Manilla.

Band of the First Colorado marching up the beach toward Manila

by noon the City of Manila would be bombarded by the Americans. This declaration was the signal for all foreign ships to withdraw to points of safety beyond possible lines of fire, and there was a general heaving of anchor and steaming away. Only the English fleet commanded by Admiral Sir Edward Chichester disobeyed. As we drew into battle-line his fleet followed, keeping within a few cable-lengths of our line, their ships all manned as though in review, and their band playing American airs.

Half a dozen broadsides from our ships cleared a path for our soldiers, through which they marched waist-deep in water, firing as they advanced. It was an exultant onset. They took seven thousand prisoners, and when our colors broke, it should have been the *Olympia* to fire the first gun, but the English, just as a proud parent looking on at the graduation exercises of its offspring, clapped his hands before the diploma was fairly in his son's grasp. So, the deep-voiced cannon of our mother country boomed the first salute to America's flag flying over Manila.

It was a glorious victory, quickly followed by a cablegram from Washington commanding a cessation of hostilities, an opportunity that our admiral embraced to get us all back into shipshape once more.

Singly and in pairs each ship returned to Hong Kong and the Kau-lung dry-docks. When our turn came, the flag with its accompanying ensign moved temporarily over to the *Baltimore*, and we rode out under the pennant of a new captain.

A bit of circumstantial evidence I am inserting here in order to prove that said new captain was proud of his berth.

It was early on our first morning out that I chanced to get a view of him. He was wearing pink pajamas and a benignant smile. In his hand was a brimming cocktail, which he lifted to his reflection in the mirror, saying in a voice that I could not help but hear, "D— us American sailors! Here's to us." Then he drained the glass.

It was only a little conceit that might be passed with a smile, but I am not alone in the opinion that, after all the hardships we had endured, including three months without shore-liberty, twenty-four hours at Hong Kong would have been no stretch of generosity on his part. The crews of the ships that had preceded us had been given it even up to forty-eight hours; in fact, it was their recital of the courteous reception tendered them by everybody in Hong Kong that awoke us to the realization of what heroes we are.

The boys on the *Charlie* are so sore not to have been in it that they could not without self-humiliation show much homage, and the "gravel agitators" [soldiers] nursed the thought all the way out here that we were unable to do anything until they came to show us how.

But in Hong Kong, the Scotch Brigade, West Yorkshire, and the Queen's Own vied with one another doing us homage, while the British sailors received us like brothers. These were the conditions awaiting us in Victoria, and we were granted only a measly overnight liberty to enjoy it.

The starboard had the second liberty, and as we gathered to return in the morning someone called out, "Come on, let's break liberty!" The way the suggestion took, one unacquainted might have thought it original. There were one hundred and sixty of us in the bunch, mostly over-timers, and a corporal's guard could not have been mustered from the gang (all ship-overs) who returned on time.

Two days later, when the *Olympia's* whistle blew a general recall, a few more, grown faint hearted, obeyed its summons, while more than one hundred of us watched our good ship sail away.

Of course there was a reward upon each head, but not a man who wore her Majesty's uniform could be bribed to lay hand upon a *hero!*

Our ship out of sight, we took up a tarpaulin muster, moved out to Happy Valley and set up camp. We were wearing our best suits, and feeling that they were not appropriate camping-togs, bought cheap white trousers and shirts and ceased to be sailors until, warned that *time* was approaching, we dressed as for muster, went in a body, and sat down outside of the U. S. Consulate and waited until it was just nine days and twenty-three hours from the time we had left the ship. Then we reported ourselves *"Stragglers*, clean and sober."

It was up to the consul to look shocked and to make a speech. This he delivered in a manner that brought him vociferous cheering. He finished by warning us to stay out by ourselves, bothering no one, and to report to him every morning between eight and ten and receive our allowance. (A silver dollar each.)

This, in addition to what was left in the tarpaulin, put us on easy-deck, though it allowed no surplus for riotous living.

We were unquestionably the attraction of Hong Kong. Hundreds of people, representatives from all classes of society, flocked to see us, and one morning, as we were on our way to the Consulate (we wore our uniforms on these trips), we met a victoria, its sole occupant being a most charming old lady. She poked her parasol into her coachman's neck as a signal to stop. It was written in her face that she wanted to say something kind and motherly to us, so she prefaced whatever she was about to say with, "Are you the American sailors?"

Before any one had time to get his cap off to answer, Jack Weir's de profundis growled, "What in h—l do you suppose we are wearing these uniforms for?"

Now, it is an established fact that, no matter how varied are the sins of the United States blue jacket, he has carved for himself a reputation, if not really for gallantry toward the gentle sex, it is something that runs parallel to that virtue. No one has ever known a sailor to stoop to what is commonly called "mashing"; in short, when on shore Jack attends strictly to his own business.

Even Weir, who has a reputation to live up to, would not have taken the initiative; but this was not the first time his answer had brought confusion and mortification to his shipmates.

Almost every evening we gave either exhibitions in boxing and wrestling or a concert, and we should have gone away leaving a record for peace equal to the one we had made for fighting on the first of May, had we not come in contact with some of the Kaiser's sailors. They were in no manner aggressive, but we were boiling with memories of Germany's treatment of us at Cavite, and we lost no occasion for taking the poor revenge that was left to us. The bloody altercations that ensued were growing irritating to the square-heads, who, resolving upon putting an end to them, sent to their ship for recruits.

We got on to their racket, and when they rowed up to the wharf we would not allow them to land. It was a bloody battle, and when it was done I stood amidst the victors watching a gory, disheveled lot of Germans pulling for their ship. Then I surveyed myself and found that the only rag that covered me from the waist up was a black ribbon on my right arm which was marked in gilt letters, *Kaiserin Augusta.*

In due time the *Concord* came in and there were rejoicings over the meeting of old friends, although they each and all intimated that all sorts of undesirable things were waiting for us in Manila.

Finally, there came a day when we went for our plunk, when the consul told us to come no more, but to be at the dock the next morning, as we were to return on the *Concord.* Oh, joy unspeakable! A trip from Hong Kong to Manila without a stroke of work! The thought was intoxicating, but we sobered quickly when we got on board, being put directly on duty while the *Concord's* crew slept all night in their hammocks, and, like passengers, laughed at us all day, not omitting to remind us that hammocks made delightful places to sleep; for we, alas! when off duty must drop on the bare decks. We worked like seamen with the accommodations of tramps.

If the captain who held sticks on the *Olympia* on our return had been less irate I think I should have turned back a few pages and drawn a blue pencil through that pajama sketch I made; but he did score us unmercifully. He has promised on the sacredness of all of his gold lace never to forget a man of us. He feels we have irredeemably disgraced the great American navy and that it is up to him to avenge it.

From our ranks the brig drew a full complement, but I was put directly back on duty in the admiral's launch. The admiral, bless him! is so very busy with a great many things that I fancy he really has forgotten if he ever heard what an escapade one hundred and one blue-jackets have been having.

Chapter XXVI

It was like returning to school after vacation. In a very few days we all settled back into our regular grooves, performing our tasks like so many automatons. Double watches and garrison duty were things of the past. We enjoyed once more the old delights of port life. General Merritt is on his way to Paris to participate in the Peace Conference, and we seem to be only waiting.

Small-arm practice makes a delightful pastime, and there is only one better shot with a pistol than Dewey, and that is freckled-face Pete of Texas. Pete is a newcomer, and the first time we had rifle target practice he made some shots that his division officer complimented. Pete replied, "Oh, I ain't much shucks with a gun, but I'm jist pizen with a pistol," and he made good his boast that he could make Buffalo Bill or the glass-ball shooters appear like amateurs in his class.

Manila is ours, and we are getting as much out of it in the way of pleasure as we are capable of. Our soldiers hold the fort and do the martyr act.

If the volunteer soldier amounts to a hill of beans after this business is over it won't be the fault of the ladies of America. Every ship that comes is ballasted with sewing bags and red flannel belly-bands, each neatly folded about a couplet of verse or a temperance tract, for the soldiers.

We are not envious, we do not want nor need their gifts, and to be just, will own that a sailor's life in Manila is not half so arduous as that of the soldier; for while we are sleeping well housed between decks, they, poor devils, are often lying in muddy trenches with a deluging rain their only canopy.

There is a veritable colony of Associated Press representatives here, and the folks at home are reading every word they write. I hope they will describe the "dusky señoritas" who sit all day beneath the shade of the palms dispensing beer from square kegs packed about with ice and garlanded with blossoms. It is quite as novel and a much prettier picture than that made by the police.

Of the latter I have never known one to make an arrest. They are the very acme of the land of *mañana*. To see policemen barefoot and ragged, carrying cocks under their arms whenever they meet, stretching themselves on the ground, listlessly watching until the bout is over, when each cop picks up his bird and goes on his beat—I say it is too funny.

At first the newness of things rendered it interesting, but when Thanksgiving came about, I searched my heart, and found the most genuine thankfulness there was that I had been born an American. With this burst of gratitude written to my own credit I drifted with the tide of events until one night, just after we had turned in, Chalmers came to my hammock and said:

"Jack, you are drafted for home, and on to the *Nero* tomorrow."

The Dewey Medal.

"Go to blazes!" I said.

"Sure, Jack; it is straight goods." But I could not believe it.

Seven months had gone by since the battle and not a man had been sent home. I lay and thought as hard as the weather would permit me to think, and, finally, when the breathing from the long rows of hammocks grew into a regular cadence, dropped from mine and ran lightly forward to the bulletin board. Could I believe my eyes? There were forty-nine names on the draft, and mine third on the list.

I shouted and I yelled. The officer-of-the-deck sent for me and would have put me into the brig for disturbing the ship's slumber, but when I told him the cause he excused me, as he did also from the watch.

I was told that I might sleep all night; but though I believe I lay as motionless as the guns in their sponsons, I never closed my eyes.

At nine o'clock in the morning I went over the side, Andy, ever faithful, helping me with my diddy-box and bag. There followed a few busy days in making ready, and, finally, one evening, when the effulgent splendor of a tropical sunset hung its banner for a background, the *Olympia's* band came on deck, and a homeward-bounder broke from the *Nero's* mainmast as the blessed strains of "Home, Sweet Home" floated into the twilight; then I threw my cap into the water and put my hands to my mouth, shouting, *"Goodbye, Andy!"* and thought I heard through the din an answering, "Aye, aye, Jack."

The piston-rods slid slow at first and then, with four bells and a jingle, the engineer threw open the throttle and away we went. I stood upon the deck looking back.

Inside the Golden Gate again.

It was the moment I had waited and prayed for, and still I was not glad. For three years and eight months the proud ship had been my home; and it was with a sickening, sinking feeling I watched it fading and fading, a leaden streak that dwindled into a black spot against a lurid sky, and I wondered when and where I should ever see her again.

We are taking back a lot of Spanish cannon, Mauser rifles, cartridges, etc., as trophies of war.

Our voyage must have been void of interest or incident but for three little occurrences. The first happened on our tenth day out. We had not sighted land for days, and were therefore not a little surprised to see a snow-white dove perched upon one of our yard-arms, where it remained throughout the forenoon; then, spreading its wings, it swooped down, circled above our heads and darted away landward.

Scotty Ross says it was no dead sailor, or it would have been a seabird. We want to bet that the Peace Treaty was signed in Paris on the tenth of December.

The second event was a typhoon that washed our chicken-coops overboard, thereby robbing us of a portion of our intended Christmas dinner; but fate or the skipper directed our course in such a manner that we got stuck on the meridian, and had two Christmas days instead of one. We were compensated for the loss of fowl by being served with plum-duff on both festivals. Duff at sea is no longer a mixture of flour and water boiled into the consistency of molten lead, and eaten with black molasses, but has evolved into a very good plum pudding.

The third and last event worth mention occurred less

than a week ago.

Dozing in the rigging, I was startled into wakefulness to find myself lying flat against the mast, face down, looking straight into the bowels of the deep; then the stern settled back and with a wallow surged into a chasm of ocean left by a mountain of water that rolled on like a single chord, struck, all out of tune, from a Wagnerian tempest.

A general summons was blown, but before all hands could muster the ship had righted herself, and there was naught to see save a blue sea hurrying on ahead. The deck officer confirmed our suppositions—it was a tidal wave.

VALE

"If you take the glasses and go aloft you ought to see the Farallones," said the *Nero's* executive officer; and, sure enough, there they were! Oh, the sight of them! It brought on a flood of memories that all but engulfed me. I tried to recall "What might have been," but it was futile. I hurried below to gather my belongings and to finish my writing, and now, sitting on my diddy-box with my book on my knee, I have only time to write that *I would rather have been in the Battle of Manila than to have sat in the United States Senate.*

On the crimson path of the setting sun we are sailing in through the Golden Gate. In another hour the bo's'n will pipe: "Take in your foresail, mainsail, and spanker, and make them up for a full do. Do you h-e-a-r that, now?" My head and my heart are throbbing; my hand trembles and my eyes grow dim.

Tomorrow I shall go ashore and take up the thread where it was broken; but if ever the American eagle shrieks for help I shall be among the first to answer, and if any one seek me, let him look, for he will surely find me—

BEHIND THE GUNS.

If you enjoyed this book, you may also be interested in these other high-quality works from Arx Publishing...

Angels in Iron by Nicholas C. Prata
"Although I trusted that the story would be fast-paced, I doubted it would engage my short attention span for that long. Starting early on a Saturday morning, I planned to read for only a couple of hours. Instead, I ended up spending the entire day reading *Angels in Iron*; the book was impossible to put down. As Prata vividly described the perilous progression of one of the most fascinating battles ever, my daily routine was shoved aside....A thrilling read, and especially recommended for boys age eleven and up.".".
— *The Kolbe Academy Little Home Journal*

Belisarius: The First Shall Be Last by Paolo A. Belzoni
"A superb ancient Rome tale that brings to life one of the last great generals of the empire....Teens and adults will appreciate this spotlight on the sixth century Roman Empire at a time when the empire—and in some chronicles of the time, the world—was on the brink of collapse as cultures collide."
—**Harriet Klausner, #1 Reviewer on Amazon.com**

Centurion's Daughter by Justin Swanton
"This was not a book dashed off and rushed to publication but something that had been lovingly labored over....First of all, let me say, I loved it....I strongly recommend this book and would say it is appropriate for young ladies and gentleman 15 years and older and their parents of course. This would be a great Christmas gift, Confirmation gift for your Confirmandi or addition to a High School Curriculum."
—**Latin Mass Network**

Crown of the World: Knight of the Temple by Nathan Sadasivan
"*Knight of the Temple* is written in a style of historical fiction that was prevalent in American Catholic literature several decades ago and follows in the footsteps of such Catholic classics as *The Outlaws of Ravenhurst* and the novels of Louis de Wohl, but with greater intensity. *Knight of the Temple* is a really excellent work, fraught with tension."
—*Saint Austin Review*

Leave If You Can by Luise Rinser
"Not your ordinary love-and-war story....It is the remarkable story of Angelina, who was first blinded by fanaticism and shaken by the injustices and atrocities of the War. After suffering and losing so much during her political and spiritual struggles, Angelina discovers that the fight for justice and human rights is found at a higher level with God as the Supreme Commander."
—*Time with Tannia Book Reviews*

For further information on these titles, or to order, visit:
www.arxpub.com

CPSIA information can be obtained
at www.ICGtesting.com
Printed in the USA
BVOW03s1119200917
495391BV00022B/50/P